Desert Screen

Desert Screen

WAR AT THE SPEED OF LIGHT

PAUL VIRILIO

Translated by

MICHAEL DEGENER

continuum
LONDON • NEW YORK

Continuum

The Tower Building, 11 York Road, London SE1 7NX

370 Lexington Avenue, New York, NY 10017-6503

www.continuumbooks.com

© The Athlone Press 2002

First published in France 1991 under the title *L'Ecran du désert*

© Editions Galilée 1991

The publishers wish to record their thanks to the French Ministry of Culture
for a grant towards the cost of translation.

British Library Cataloguing-in-Publication Data

A catalogue record for this book is available from the British Library.

ISBN 0-8264-5821-1 (hardback)
0-8264-5822-X (paperback)

Library of Congress Cataloging-in-Publication Data

Virilio, Paul.
  [Ecran du désert English]
  Desert screen : war at the speed of light / Paul Virilio ; translated by
Michael Degener.
      p. cm. — (Athlone contemporary European thinkers)
  Includes bibliographical references and index.
  ISBN 0-8264-5821-1 — ISBN 0-8264-5822-X (pbk.)
  1. Operation Desert Shield, 1990–1991, in mass media. I. Title. II. Series.

DS79.739.V5713 2002
956.7044′2—dc21   2001042538

Typeset by Acorn Bookwork, Salisbury, Wiltshire
Printed and bound in Great Britain by
The Cromwell Press, Trowbridge, Wiltshire

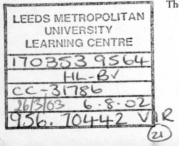

Contents

Acknowledgements

I would like to thank Lauren Osepchuk for her assistance with translation and correspondence, also Benjamin de Vulpillieres, Mark Koontz and Max Statkiewicz for assistance with some thorny questions. William Arken assisted with some technical matters, and I am grateful to Martha Loomis for her ever-gracious editorial suggestions. I extend special thanks to my editor Tristan Palmer for his fine suggestions and patience throughout.

Finally, I am grateful to Paul Virilio not only for sharing his decennial reflections, but for having been 'there', albeit as a telespectator, ten years ago as a voice in the wilderness, a voice in the desert . . .

Michael Degener
Northampton, Massachusetts

Preface

A war of pictures and sounds is replacing the war
of objects (projectiles and missiles). In a techni-
cian's version of an all-seeing Divinity, ever
ruling out accident and surprise, the drive is on
for a general system of illumination that will
allow everything to be seen and known, at every
moment and in every place.

> Paul Virilio, *War and Cinema: The Logistics of
> Perception* (1984)

Three months ago, they weren't seeing us. But
suddenly, they were. Something was different.

> A senior Pentagon official, 'US and British Jets
> Strike Air-Defense Centers in Iraq', *New York
> Times*, 17 February 2001

Time has been kind to one of its most corrosive critics, Paul
Virilio. The acceleration of technological change, the
collapse of politics into media event, the melding of war
and cinema, the threat of a networked accident, the oblit-
eration of space itself: all these speed-effects were diagnosed
before their time by Virilio. Many of his most hyperbolic
statements now seem tame compared to, say, a *Wall Street
Journal* article on the volatility of the market, or a Pentagon
official speaking out on the national security threat posed by
hackers. The Virilio corpus, a remarkable output of twenty
major works in just over two decades, provides a litany for

vii

the end of a century as well as a series of prophecies for the beginnings of a new one.

It is always dangerous to distil a complex writer, and for such a theoretically intensive and empirically rich thinker, a version of 'Virilio Lite' is like foam without the beer, taste without the kick. Besides, as anyone who has read Virilio would testify, it is just about syntactically impossible. However, for the benefit of newcomers to Virilio, I offer chapter without verse of his key thoughts and concepts.[1] And to the delight of Virilio veterans (I hope), *Desert Screen* is rounded off by a short interview with the author on the legacy of the Gulf War.

The primary preoccupation of Virilio, what he considers to be the signifying moment of modernity, is the coeval emergence of a mass media and an industrial army, where the capability to war without war manifests a parallel information market of propaganda, illusion, dissimulation. Technological accelerants like satellite link-ups, real-time feeds and high-resolution video augment the power of television not just to dissimulate but to substitute whole realities in time as well as space. With the appearance of a global view comes the disappearance of the viewer-subject: in the immediacy of perception, our eyes become indistinguishable from the camera's optics, and critical consciousness, along with the body, goes missing.

From now on everything passes through the image. The image has priority over the thing, the object, and sometimes even the physically-present being. Just as real time, instantaneousness, had priority over space. There-

deterritorialization + eradication of social, political of cultural practices from their native places

fore the image is invasive and ubiquitous. Its role is not to be in the domain of art, the military domain or the technical domain, it is to be everywhere, to be reality ... I believe that there is a war of images ... And I can tell you my feelings in another way: winning today, whether it's a market or a fight, is merely not losing sight of yourself.[2]

From his earliest writings Virilio deploys critical concepts for understanding this escalating war of images. Future conflicts would be decided not in the various nations' foreign ministries or on the battlefield, but in the electro-magnetic spectrum of informational, *cybernetic wars* of persuasion and dissuasion. He introduces terms like *deterritorialization*, *nomadism* and the *suicidal state*, which Deleuze and Guattari pick up and brilliantly elaborate in their most significant work, *A Thousand Plateaus*. Never one to wallow in the anxiety of influence, Virilio takes Foucault's panopticon model to an extraterrestrial level of discipline and control, offering a micro-analysis of how new technologies of oversight and organizations of control, innovated by strategic alliances of the military, industrial and scientific communities, have made the cross-over into civilian and political sectors to create a global *administration of fear*. It is not so much the acuity and reach of Foucault's analysis that is extended by Virilio, as it is the *dimensionality*, showing how the control of space has been force-multiplied if not displaced by the control of pace. Virilio draws on Walter Benjamin's fear of an aestheticized politics, but pushes it further, to show how the politics of subjectivity, no longer

referred to medical physical biological aspects of social system

Past principle something remotely pleases

15th century, period of Italian art or architecture.

willing, no longer able to maintain representational distinctions between the real, the visual and the virtual, *disappears into the aesthetic*. This disappearance is facilitated by a melding of military, cinematic and techno-scientific *logistics of perception*. All economies of sight and might, remnants of presence like quattrocento linear fields of perception, national-territorial politics, Cartesian subjectivity, Newtonian physics, become coordinated, and eventually subordinated, by a relativist, quantum, *transpolitical* war machine. In political terms, this means that the geopolitics of *extensivity* and *exo-colonization* is displaced by the *chronopolitics* of *intensivity* and *endo-colonization*. In turn, episodic war gives way, through the infinite requirements and preparations of deterrence and simulations, to a permanent, logistical *pure war*.

name given to the philosophical and scientific system of René Descartes

how we are losing grip on what human mean

Virilio's rapid-fire, *fin-de-siècle* assessments intended (among other things) to shock us into the realization that the triumphalism of the end of the Cold War masked a critical transformation of pure war, from a nuclear state of war without warring to a non-nuclear, information-infused form of global dissuasion and compulsion. His early warnings were vindicated in 1991 by the first conventionally fought pure war, the Desert Shield air campaign and the 100-hour Desert Storm ground war that followed. His analysis of the Gulf War, much of it originally published in newspapers and other French periodicals during the war, was collected and published as *Desert Screen*. Today it practically reads like folklore, almost as a gnostics for the early non-believers of pure war.

Early knowledge

It is especially illuminating — in the radar-targeting sense captured by Virilio and the 'senior Pentagon official' at the beginning of this introduction – to read *Desert Screen* in the context of the official events surrounding the ten-year anniversary of the Gulf War 'victory'. Designated 'National Security Week' by the new President Bush, it featured Senate hearings, the announcement of a top-to-bottom defence review and a series of presidential addresses at military bases, all accompanied by a burst of Great Power chest-beating, flag-waving patriotism, and sentimental testimonials to past and future sacrifices. However, in this media storm, not everything went according to script. Tragic accidents marred two separate military events in Hawaii: the submarine USS *Greeneville*, playing theme-park ride to a group of visiting civilians from Texas, executed an emergency surface manoeuvre that sank a Japanese fishing ship on a training cruise, killing five sailors and four students; and in the 'Lightning Thrust Warrior' exercise, two UH-60 Black Hawk helicopters collided, killing six soldiers. Once again, Virilio anticipates such events, where the accident serves as diagnostic of cultural differences as well as the negation of new technologies, as a caesura of progress as well as warning sign for the techno-fetishist.

Intended as a precision-guided message to old enemies, potential foes and the American public, the initial reviews of National Security Week were decidedly mixed. However, with a finale of twenty-four US and British warplanes attacking five separate Iraqi air defence stations, no amount of background noise could drown out the signal emanating from the military-industrial-media-entertainment network: pure war up and running again.

The National Security Week was full of *information bombs*, a Virilio expression adapted from Einstein for the explosive effect of living in networked real time, where the immediacy of events and collapse of cause and effect valorizes speed, cybernetic reflex and crisis management over human reflection and deliberative decision-making. Emanating from the fastest centres of power and targeting the slower periphery, information bombs are putatively efficient and discriminate. The first bomb was delivered by the head of the CIA, George Tenet, speaking to the Senate Select Committee on Intelligence on the worldwide threats facing the USA today:

> As I reflect this year, Mr Chairman, on the threats to American security, what strikes me most forcefully is the *accelerating pace of change* [original italics] in so many arenas that affect our nation's interests. Numerous examples come to mind: new communications technology that enables the efforts of terrorists and narcotraffickers as surely as it aids law enforcement and intelligence, *rapid* global population growth that will create new strains in parts of the world least able to cope, the weakening internal bonds in a number of states whose cohesion can no longer be taken for granted, the *breaking down of old barriers to change* in places like the Koreas and Iran, the *accelerating* growth in missile capabilities in so many parts of the world − to name just a few.[3]

The second bomb came a few days later, when President Bush spoke at Fort Stewart, Georgia. To a round of 'hoo-ahs' (the infantry's version of applause) he announced:

In a world of *fast-changing threats*, you give us stability. Because of you, America is secure. Because of you, the march of freedom continues ... Our nation can never fully repay our debt to you, but we can give you our full support. And my administration will.[4]

The following day the President headed for the US Joint Forces Command in Norfolk, Virginia, to virtually participate in a battle simulation of a combined naval and land attack in Europe. The President was video-linked to the USS *Mount Whitney*, a command and control ship about 40 miles off Virginia Beach, so that he could watch and participate through three over-sized screens that used three-dimensional radar images to display every ship, missile and aircraft in, under and over the Atlantic. In the opening lines of the speech that followed he dropped the third bomb, temporally defining the blast radius *before* spatially identifying just who and where the future enemy might be:

Eleven years after the Cold War, we are in a time of *transition and testing*, when it will be decided what dangers draw near or pass away, what tragedies are invited or averted. We must use this time well. We must *seize this moment*.

The bulk of the speech was a straightforward endorsement of pure war, explicitly linking the possibilities for peace to the military's ability to harness the technological revolution in information and surveillance, simulation and speed, and to deploy it as a conventional deterrent against all possible comers:

We must extend our peace by advancing our technology. We are witnessing a *revolution* in the technology war. Power is increasingly defined not by size but *by mobility and swiftness*. Advantage increasingly comes from information, such as the three-dimensional images of simulated battle that I have just seen. Safety is gained in stealth and forces projected on the long arc of precision-guided weapons.[5]

And to punctuate his view that virtue and peace are on the side of superior fire-power, President Bush added to the written speech a personal benediction: 'God Bless NATO.'

After that he was off to Mexico to meet the new President Vincente Fox, and, in the midst of informal talks about drugs, migration and allowing Californians to tap into the Mexican electrical grid, US and British war planes — without the rest of a God-blessed NATO — dropped their real bombs on the Iraqi air defence network. The two presidents held an outdoor press conference, where President Bush declared that 'it was a routine mission', taking care to let all know that it was one 'about which I was informed and I authorized'.[6] The USA and the rest of the world were put on notice that there was a new sheriff in town, one well versed in pure war and well equipped with a full arsenal of information bombs.

From the *data coup d'état* in the Florida presidential elections to the *cathodic democracy* of Bush redux to the *media-staged strategic event* in Iraq, Virilio's concepts act as a kind of critical bunker for all the falling bombs. Ten years after Desert Storm, we face a new electromagnetic maelstrom with familiar faces at the helm: President George W. Bush (son of then President George Bush), Vice President Richard Cheney (then Secretary of Defense), Secretary of State Colin Powell (then Chairman of the Joint Chiefs of Staff). Karl Marx, on the effort by Napoleon III to re-establish the French Empire, said: first time tragedy, second time farce. One emerges from National Security Week suspecting a worse turn of the screw: first time pure war, second time . . . IT'S *SATURDAY NIGHT LIVE*, hosted by George 'Dubya' Bush, with special musical guests from the Cold War, 'The Undead'. Reason enough to read, one more time before time runs out, *Desert Screen*.

James Der Derian,
Princeton, NJ, February 2001

POSTSCRIPT

One year after James Der Derian's preface, and with this book in final proofs, Virilio's 1991 prognostications resurface with a renewed relevance. Once again it would seem Iraq is coming into the line of fire, sighted on George Bush's newly defined 'axis of evil'. Yet just as Bush redefines the latest brand of Evil Empire, his would-be allies — in what is being referred to this time as *America's* New War on terrorism — threaten to peel off from the fragile 'coalition'. So, after this one momentous year, are we prepared to return abruptly to Bush's post-inaugural, anti-internationalist stance, as if the horror of 9/11 and the need for a *world* response have already somehow been superseded? With another Gulf War looming, some nightmarish repetition syndrome, a media replay, threatens. Will it be again, as Virilio analysed it then, an American-led 'techno-fundamentalist' coalition squaring off against a resurgent Muslim religious fundamentalism? Or will Saddam Hussein this time face a *new* George Bush, now leading the US more or less alone into what he called a 'crusade'? Will we be reminded of Virilio's curious fascination with the palindrome 1991 by the next palindrome in sequence, 2002?

Michael Degener
Boston, MA, February 2002

NOTES

1. More detailed versions can be found in my introduction to *The Virilio Reader*, Oxford: Blackwell Publishers, 1998; and 'The Conceptual Cosmology of Paul Virilio', *Theory, Culture & Society*, Fall, 1999.
2. See Virilio interview in *Block 14*, Autumn, 1988, pp. 4–7.
3. George J. Tenet, 'Worldwide Threat 2001: National Security in a Changing World', statement made before the Senate Select Committee on Intelligence, 7 February 2001 (http://www.cia.gov/cia/public_affairs/speeches/ UNCLASWWT_02072001.html).
4. Mike Allen and Edward Walsh, 'A "Hoo-Ah!" and Some Numbers', *Washington Post*, 13 February 2001, p. 6.
5. 'Excerpts from Bush's Remarks on the Military', *New York Times*, 14 February 2001, p. A26.
6. 'In the President's Words on the Bombing: "It's a Routine Mission"', *New York Times*, 17 February 2001, p. A4.

I

Foreword

This book is the work of an attentive tele-spectator, a tele-spectator of a world war in miniature that for many long months captured the attention of a public transfixed, no longer able to believe their eyes. And then, immediately following the incredulity – the distance, the dropping-off of public opinion and, finally, the fading from memory of this conflict that paradoxically eluded everyone due to the lack of territorial scale matched by the immediacy of its presentation in the media.

At the end of his book *L'Influence de l'armement sur l'his-toire,*[1] which appeared in 1948, Major-General J. F. C. Fuller wrote, paraphrasing Lucretius, 'It is cleverness, or courage, or speed to which each animal that breathes today under the sun owes the survival of its species. *But now, in the age of atomic energy that opens before us, of these three principles, it is speed that dominates.*'

The uniqueness of the war that was just interrupted (if not completed) is in effect to have underlined this decisive acceleration, and to have finally permitted the deterrence of explosives – atomic or otherwise – to be surpassed by that of the means of their air or space delivery: the guidance, the navigation of missiles or fighter planes, but above all the pinpointing of targets and the jamming of enemy transmissions, blocking all significant action of the adversary's forces.

Henceforth, the instantaneous speed of the transmission of data, as well as the extreme precision of the guidance and navigation of projectiles, will surpass the destructive power of conventional or non-conventional arms.

The very long period of the supremacy of *defence* over *offence* that marked the history of fortification through the course of the ages, and finally ceded its place, with the rise of artillery, to the offensive, and therefore to the supremacy of the war of movement over the war of siege — all leading up to the appearance of the atomic bomb — is superseded today by the era of the supremacy of the *absolute speed* of weapons of interdiction on the field of battle over the movement of the *relative speeds* of mechanized forces.

Therefore we must not deceive ourselves, for despite the development of air–land military units using 'forward projection' — such as the American Rapid Deployment Force (RDF), which was the source of the success of the Gulf War thanks to its logistical capacities, or even the French Force d'action rapide (FAR)[2] and the Rapid Reaction Force (RRF), comprising the future military means of NATO forces stationed in Europe — the essence of the strategy is to be found elsewhere in the extraterrestrial components of the US Strategic Defence Initiative, the orbital deployment of independent satellite or reconnaissance forces, of advance alert or transmission, depending solely upon 'the American spatial high command', a true *deus ex machina* of planetary peace or war.

Meanwhile, the very name 'strategic defence', the Pentagon's term for that which others more imaginatively named 'Star Wars', reveals the fundamentally ambiguous character of these *arms of interdiction on the field of battle* that not only intend to extend deterrence by other, non-nuclear, means but also to prohibit any large-scale action of this or that land force, thus effecting a sort of paralysis, a geostrategic inertia, under the control of the USA, but also under the Soviet Union.

It is thus foolish to allow ourselves to be duped any longer by the outdated arguments of military leaders concerning the anti-crisis capacities of different means of putatively 'rapid' action or reaction; the most important thing is located elsewhere, above our heads, beyond the stratosphere, in that circumterrestrial void where a terrifying number of non-flying and barely identifiable objects circulate: those communications weapons of a fourth front, henceforth dominating the other three, those of the earth, sea and air, and whose sovereign power resides in the emission and reception of electromagnetic waves, radio-electric signals or even lasers, all operating at the speed of light.

'*Where we find the tanks, there is the front,*' declared Heinz Guderian, the blitzkrieg warrior from the 1940s. Now this statement is outdated, replaced by the following: '*Where we find the satellites, there is the fourth front.*' This is the front of the weapons of communication, of instantaneous information or destruction, cancelling all military power over both the earth and sky, to the advantage of this other-world where the Great Automaton reigns.

To paraphrase J. F. C. Fuller's remarks concerning the attack tank, from now on we can say: 'Following the example of the mobile fortress that unites all the advantages of protection from the battle of siege or position and all the offensive powers of the field artillery, *the military satellite revolutionized the art of war between 1990 and 1991.*'[3]

Let us not misinterpret this conflict, nor be caught lagging behind this war. The victory of coalition air forces in the Gulf War does not amount to the end of the land army as superseded by an air power that itself superseded the naval power of the past; but rather to the future of a weapons system of a literally 'exorbitant' power, where the speed of communication and instantaneous guidance of trajectories of destruction from space annihilate every offensive capacity based on movement, on the attack of mechanized land forces.

The *tyranny of real time* is therefore not an empty phrase, since it concerns just as much the power of the major states as the purely political power of nations engaged in a major historical confrontation following the end of the Cold War between the East and the West; nations that find themselves, suddenly, destitute and paralysed by an 'umbrella' less nuclear than satellitar [*satellitaire*][4] that was supposed to protect against all aggression, and that results today in the means to a total control the scale of which had previously been suggested only by meteorology.

It is easy to see that the 1992 'Open Sky' treaty of Europe is largely implicated in this geostrategic transmutation. In fact, the new strategy of NATO is now centred just as much on the management of regional crises as on defence against a surprise attack by the Soviet Union, today considered highly improbable.

The rejection, pure and simple, of the old American concept of a 'flexible response' corresponds to the idea of the use of atomic weapons as a *last recourse*. Thus the decline of a properly nuclear deterrent is confirmed (if there were still any doubt), as it is now replaced by the latest type of interdiction based on an orbital power jointly instituted, we should note, by the Russians and the Americans.

European autonomy with respect to the USA in questions of defence, so important to the French, whatever the political orientation of the various governments, is therefore less and less likely. The British are even preparing, with the consent of their Atlantic partners, to take over the command of the future rapid reaction force.

Let us point out then, by way of a provisional conclusion, that the Persian Gulf War was not won by Europe, and this despite the significant intervention by France on the side of the allies. The articles that follow illustrate a series of illusions carefully maintained by the means of information that used and abused their live audience, a manipulated public, where the recent loss of credibility of the mass media is the measure of this *strategy of deception*, to which, to differing degrees, we have all been, more often than not, consenting victims.

FROM THE POTENTIAL WAR TO THE PROBABLE CITY

To say that the City and War go hand in glove is a euphemism. The city, the *polis*, is constitutive of the form of conflict called WAR, just as war is itself constitutive of the political form called the CITY. Even if tribal conflicts, the turmoil of nomadic and prehistoric origins, represented a tactical prefiguration of the conflict organized by sedentary societies, we must await the rise of urban civilization for real war to emerge from the historical development of the city.

Indeed, before being its actual perpetration, the political conflict is first its economic preparation, I would even say its strategic premonition. But this sort of military anticipation will first be associated with the management of the 'theatre of operation', with this training ground where war will actually take place.

Where the hunter's snares and traps anticipated the movement and the fall of game, war will anticipate, in its turn, the movement of troops, their momentum, their course and finally their halting in place. From this arises the decisive importance of the urban territory, of its limits and its ways of access like a 'training field for manoeuvres', to this strategic thinking that was confused from the start with the political reasoning of the leader of the city, at once mayor and military leader, 'strategist'[5] of the ancient city.

If there are three major epochs of real war – the tactical and prehistorical epoch consisting of limited violence and confrontations; then the strategic epoch, historical and purely political; and finally, the contemporary and transpolitical logistical epoch, where science and industry play a determining role in the destructive power of opposing forces – there are also three great types of weapons that progress in importance through the course of the ages, in the age-old duel between offensive and defensive forces: weapons of obstruction (ditches, ramparts, bastions, armour and fortresses of all sorts); weapons of destruction (lances, bows, cannons, machine-guns, missiles, etc.); and finally, weapons of communication (lookout towers and signals, information and transport carriers, optical telegraph, wireless telephone, radar and satellites, among others).

For each of these weapons a particular type of confrontation dominates: the war of siege for the first, the war of movement for the second and the all-out blitzkrieg [*guerre éclair et totalitaire*] for the last.

Moreover, for each of the decisive weapons, there was, in its time, a specific 'mode of deterrence'. The city surrounded by a fortified ring long deterred attacks by siege, up to the invention of artillery capable of destroying its walls. The war of movement, which succeeded techniques of encirclement, reached its limit with the innovation of strategic bombing equipped with atomic weapons.

And thereupon followed the nuclear deterrence between the East and West in the wake of the destruction of the cities of Hiroshima and Nagasaki.

Before analysing further the recent development of the new 'real-time' weapons of communication, arising from what, during the course of the Cold War, were long called 'counter-value[6] strategies', let us return again to the very origin of the 'political war' − that mode of war of which Clausewitz made himself the apostle and theoretician. An important fact prevails: if the synoecism of the tribes composing the Greek city led finally to rites of autochthony,[7] that is, to the means for integrating strangers, it is because the nascent city (Athens, as it happens) first defined itself by reference to the latent threat of civil war. This stasis[8] (metastasis) will later explain the advent of the rights of citizens[9] and the rise of the political-citizen as soldier-citizen, a free man who could initiate an *agon* and therefore give up his life for his rights, the no-man's land of neighbouring territories being the place of non-rights, the space of exile, of ostracization.

Just as the enclosure of the city protected it from its external enemies, so also was it fortified against the enemy within, clans whose politico-military unity threatened to explode at any moment. This double challenge to the urban order explains the appearance of the public place (agora, forum), at once a 'political stage' for democratic confrontations and a 'staging ground' for the mobilization of soldier-citizens before they would head out, united, to defend the gates and walls of the urban fortification.

A double construction of a theatre of military operation: first, on the ramparts and beyond, at the foot of the walls of the city – on this glacis that would later become the suburb, the exterior [*la banlieue*], the place of exclusion [*le lieu des bannis*] from the rights of the citizen – and second, in the heart of the city, with its agora, the staging ground of politics, where the battle of ideas and interests would be both concrete and metaphorical.

The later invention of the ghetto (in Venice and elsewhere) would eventually reproduce, like an echo, this phenomenon of panicked anticipation of internal war, by the management of the most populated neighbourhoods for those excluded and for those to be promoted in the future.

With the obstruction of, and later the accession to, first ownership, and then the right to vote based on census taxation, and then full citizenship, the foreigner would be put through a sort of filter that would most often prove to be a dead end, in the form of pogroms and other programmes for eliminating supernumerary groups perceived as a danger to the stability of the connective tissue of the city. Internal and external, not only within and outside the enclosure of the law, of *nomos*,[10] but interior and exterior to citizenship, that is, the active participation in the militia of citizen-soldiers who could not allow the inclusion of questionable 'comrades' – questionable because they possessed nothing to defend but their own hides, which were not worth much in the epoch of slavery.

Thus the strategic and political importance of the *miles*,[11] the ancient 'citizen-soldier' who defended his possessions, his family and the entire city, as well as his own person. And from this that chant of the *agon* where the citizen found himself already dead within the sphere of rights and law, those 'rights of the citizen' that, in surpassing him as an isolated individual, made of him a participant in the large, fundamentally political, body of the city. Thus the ghetto was, like the agora or the forum, a two-sided coin: on the one hand, a place of retreat and exclusion from the social fabric; and, on the other, a space of relative liberty for the like/unlike, foreigners as potential enemies on the way to assimilation or complete exclusion.

The sphere of the elect [*lieu d'élection*] of the city state of free men was therefore also a sphere of exclusion [*lieu d'éjection*], the engine of a pneumatic[12] democratic life that was predictably selective in the very measure to which this democracy was of the minority, the Greek city state having been a sort of island of the political in an ocean of servitude and tyranny in the ancient world.

———

Today, even if God may still need men, war does not, or just barely . . . as victims. Consider, for example, chemical weapons or the neutron bomb, which eliminate humans, the animal, but carefully preserve material objects. In fact, the metastasis so feared by the ancients has taken place. The decomposition of the social (what Leonardo Sciascia called a sicilianization, by virtue of the proliferation of clans, of sects) progresses as the enlarged family of the agrarian mode of production gives way to the nuclear family of the urban petite bourgeoisie, and finally to the contemporary form commonly called monoparental. Thus, as the city increases through the course of the ages, so the unity of the people has decreased. Henceforth useless, or nearly so, as a 'producer' (skilled or non-skilled worker . . .) or as 'destroyer' (soldier, conscript . . .), the supernumerary man of the enormous megalopolis is forced to give up his status as citizen to the dubious advantage of increasingly sophisticated substitute material: automated machine tools operated by remote control, or war machines automatically controlled by computer.[13]

In this epoch military-industrial and scientific logistics prevail over strategic doctrines and truly political arguments – war being no longer the continuation of politics by other means, according to Gorbachev. The era opens as weapons of instantaneous communication come to dominate, thanks to the rise of globalized information networks and tele-surveillance. In effect, in the logistical era of war, and contrary to the strategic era that preceded it, the power of destruction has been transferred from the armed population to weapons systems, mass killers excluding the mass of killers of the past: the soldiers of the second year of the republican calendar,[14] the soldiers of Napoleon's old guard or the allied soldiers of the last two world wars, and this beginning with the terrorist innovation of an atomic weapon capable of precluding political war ecologically, by endangering the very survival of the human race.

We enter thus into both a third era of war and a new stage of the city, or more exactly of the post-industrial meta-city. The relatively recent end of classical deterrence between the East and West, with its geopolitical uncertainties, results in the urgent necessity of reinterpreting the doctrines of military engagement, going all the way back to the most distant origins of history.

If, as Michelet asserted, each epoch dreams the next, each conflict of historical importance tends to imagine that which follows. We saw this with the First and Second World Wars leading into the era of atomic deterrence; and we will see it tomorrow with the end of the equilibrium of terror and the inauguration of a nuclear proliferation, the inception of a sudden multiplication of the 'deterrence of the strong by the weak' of which the Gulf crisis is a harbinger.

If weapons of obstruction were initially established by the city state within its ramparts, and the ghetto within the limits of a reserved quarter, and if weapons of destruction, from the age of artillery until that of the atomic bomb, were created to surpass the urban limit spread around its content, the railroad and automobile extending this dissolution, with the development most recently of 'weapons of mass communication', the political definition of the image of the city again becomes problematic.

A crucial question presents itself to those currently in power: if early warning satellites – but also telecommunications satellites – have led to the impossibility of a surprise attack on opposing territory and have thus contributed to the disarmament that is abolishing the deterrence of the strong by the strong – all the while promoting the interpenetration of different points of view throughout the world – what type of 'military' interdiction, or even just 'police' interdiction, will these weapons of instantaneous communication give rise to in the face of the proliferation of chemical or atomic weapons? The appearance of a deterrence of the strong by the weak is no longer limited to France, or Great Britain or Israel, but is rather generalized, as Iraq, Pakistan and the constantly growing list of other countries are preparing to avail themselves of the ultimate weapon.

Are we about to witness a return to inertia, to the blockade and therefore to a state of siege, as in the most distant past of the city? If we consider the role played by the United Nations throughout the course of 1990 – this is what seems most likely – we can see that all of the Security Council resolutions, which imposed embargoes first by land, then by sea and then by air, were all heading in this direction.

The bipolar deterrence between the NATO bloc and the Warsaw bloc, with its allies in the third world, was succeeded by the conception of a polar deterrence in which

the UN would play the role of a worldwide pseudogovern-
ment, with France even going so far as to propose to the
Security Council the launching of 'blue satellites'[15] to guarantee world peace.

And so, following upon the great wars of movement and
the advent of a *total war* involving the progressive militarization of science and the economy of nations, we would be
providing for a paralysis: a polar inertia of a *total peace* guaranteed by the UN.

This would mark a return to the point of departure of
history, where the 'state of siege' would again find its strategic primacy, no longer on the level of the city state, of
the threatened region or nation state, but, this time, on the
level of the entire world – while the recent development of
a protectionist ideology of ecology is heading in the direction of a definitive supremacy of a 'global security' over the
political defence of nations. We have, however, a certain
reservation with regard to what might appear to some as an
'end to history': with the logistical importance accorded to
weapons of mass communication over that of weapons of
mass destruction, the logic of war becomes paradoxical.
Everything depends henceforth on verisimilitude or the lack
thereof, information and disinformation renewing the duel
between arms and armour.

Listen to the words of Emile Gaboriau, a writer from
that nineteenth century which saw the rise of the first great
press agencies: 'As concerns the news: distrust what seems
most likely, always begin by believing what seems most
unbelievable.'

And so the era of illusion is about to make its début. The

topical character of the city of free and equal men assembled in a public place is to be succeeded by a teletopical meta-city where the public image 'in real time' will probably supplant the quite real space of cities of the republic. Harbingers of a serious conflict of interpretation between democracy and dromocracy, where the post-industrial implementation of an absolute speed (that of electromagnetic waves) will abolish the progress that arose from the accessibility to the public of relative speeds since Greco-Latin antiquity. In *The Constitution of the Athenians*, a text dating from 429 to 424 BC, we find something on the subject:

> I would say first that it is just that in Athens the poor and the people count more than the nobles and the rich: for it is the people who make the navies work and who give to the City its power. And this counts as well for the pilots, the rowing masters, the second-in-command, the lookout, and those who build the ships. It is to all of these that the City owes its force, much more than to the hoplites, or nobles, or gentlemen.[16]

In maritime democracy, contrary to Lacedemonian democracy, the power of Athens is first of all that of its vessels and not solely of its citizen-infantry — consider the importance of Piraeus and the fortification of 'long walls' between Athens and its port. Democracy, the constitution of the Athenians, is therefore also dromocratic, since those who run the navy govern the city. Contrary to traditional autocratic regimes, the division of public power is comparable to that of the power of physical displacement (such as was not the case with the ancient cavalry, in particular the *equite romani*[17]).

It would be the same in the republic of Venice, which will, appropriately, inaugurate the island of the *Ghetto Nuovo* with its apartments of approximately ten storeys. With the division of riches and especially of spoils, the Athenian democracy, like the Venetian republic, will also be founded upon the division of the speed of triremes[18] or galleys. The considerable political and cultural power of these great historic cities will thus derive literally from the propulsive capacity of a people engaged in the great movement of the acceleration of history (read Fernand Braudel!).

All of this will continue up to our day, with not only the impact of the 'labour force' of the proletariat engaged in the industrial revolution but also in the ultimately misunderstood transportation revolution that will favour the democratization of rapid movement, not only public transportation, thanks to railroads (following seafaring) and to the railroad station (following the port), but also private transportation, with the domestic automobile.

It is relative speed, on the one hand, with seafaring, the train, the car, the plane (the airport following the train station), that will permit the progressive development of an industrial democracy; while absolute speed, on the other hand, with telecommunications and tele-command (the teleport following the airport), will finally give rise to the latest of revolutions: the communications revolution that will abolish, along with distances, the very necessity of physical movement of whatever sort . . .

Can we democratize ubiquity, instantaneity; in other

words, can we democratize inertia? Such is indeed the question that presents itself today to politics, to those who tomorrow will build the 'Mediate City' [*Cité Médiate*]. After the unfortunate invasion of the private automobile, will generalized automation bring us back, through the bias of an absurd individualism, towards autocracy? A post-industrial and post-urban autocracy whose golden boys and other traders would have proven to be the clinical symptoms? Far more threatened by the 'excess speed' of tele-technologies than by the excess wealth of an apparently triumphant capitalism, will democracy finally prevail as some imagine, or on the contrary, is it simply going to disappear?

The answer to these questions is being worked out, beginning today, not only according to the civic and political plan of the rights of people to come, but especially, it would seem, according to the military and logistical plans of the war to come.

II

August 1990: Desert Shield

HOLY WAR OR PURE WAR?

Changes occur in military regimes just as they do in political regimes; the first are historically less frequent, but we are nevertheless in the presence of such a military change, which it would seem is as serious as it can be.

For nearly forty years, we have consistently been told: *the nuclear regime does not foster war but rather prevents it*. The question that presents itself today: *until when?*

Just as East–West deterrence was not limited to the confrontation between 'communism' and 'capitalism', but was directly concerned with the nature of the political economy of the globe, so also the optical illusion of a North–South conflict explains neither the nature nor the gravity of that which threatens us today. Whether we like it or not, we must analyse what is named euphemistically 'the Gulf Crisis', without reference to 'good' or 'evil', without any further reference to the different *opposing forces* [*camps en présence*], but rather with regard to two types of opposing *matériel [matériels en présence]*: chemical and atomic.

If, as the specialist in catastrophes explains so well, para-phrasing René Thom, 'that which limits the *true* is not the *false*, but the *insignificant*', we must assert today that that which separates just and unjust war is widely known to be *insignificant*, and that this began from the moment when the

17

nature of the threat overwhelmed the objective of war. Today, to act locally we must think globally; the contemporary 'ecological' strategy demands it.

Think not only of international law, of the respect for the sovereignty of one state or another, but of the necessity of a free flow of oil or the most essential commodities, and also of the unprecedented character of the risks involved: not only those of the mass extermination resulting from a chemical war on both sides of the Iraqi–Saudi border but also of the menace of the possible use of a tactical atomic weapon, beginning at that point when we will have crossed, *thanks to chemical weapons*, the fragile barrier of deterrence established for a number of years in connection with this sort of warfare.

Until now, what checked the development and the proliferation of atomic weapons was less the scientific secret of the impossibility of technical realization by certain poor countries than the impossibility of their *actual use* against an adversary also fully armed with such weapons. If this prohibition were to suddenly disappear as a result of the Gulf Crisis, we would face the risk of direct proliferation in all its forms, be it that of crude or sophisticated weapons.

When it is obvious that a weapon has become an instrument, an *operationally active tool*, no one has the means to prevent its production and possession, national or international power being in this regard completely powerless.

If Saddam Hussein were to use his chemical weapons against such adversaries as the Americans or the British (not forgetting, as well, the Russians or the French), the great nuclear powers, the operational use of atomic weapons

18

would probably be inevitable, not only on the Iraqi–Kuwaiti battlefield, but *everywhere at once*.

What we must defend is therefore not only the Saudi border, or the rights of the Kuwaiti state, but also the fragile limit that still separates the symbolic threat from its actual use.

On the symbolic level, in fact, the deterrent power of chemical vs. atomic weapons is equivalent – hence the name 'atomic bomb of the poor' given to this type of munition.

To undermine the resistance to use one of these weapons is to open the Pandora's box of the other, with the immediate devastation this presupposes; but above all, and what is probably worse, it would set in motion the proliferation of these types of weapons at the very moment when we have been planning their destruction.

Let me be clear: it is not a question here of advocating permissiveness when faced with the wrongs of a megalomaniacal leader who has no fear of igniting a war against Iran and Kuwait, and who did not hesitate to gas the Kurds in his own territory. The phrase *'Saddam Hussein is Hitler'* seems to me weak, even optimistic, as the risks associated with the Middle East in 1990 are ultimately incomparable with those of Europe in the 1940s.

If the Russians and the Americans have just ended the 'Cold War' and have together initiated a promising disarmament, it is less by reciprocal goodwill than because they were no longer masters of an arms race that ruined their economies and threatened at any time to get out of control. Listen to Gorbachev: 'The existence of nuclear weapons is laden with a permanently unpredictable risk. The global situation could become such that it would no longer depend upon politics, but rather become captive to chance' (in *Perestroika*).

In this case in particular, the change of a military regime gives rise to a political shift in the sense of a *coup d'état*, solely by the historical weight of the change in the nature of power (we saw it long ago with maritime power, for example). The change in regime that threatens us today threatens not only international law, and territorial or democratic legitimacy, precisely when the latter has become in vogue nearly everywhere, but threatens also the economy of geopolitical and strategic thinking with the exorbitant risk of a generalized military anarchy, signalled by the proliferation of atomic and chemical weapons.

In fact, *the Gulf Crisis is the test case of the deterrence of the strong by the weak*, for it has blurred the very utility of deterrence between the strongest, i.e., the East and the West. France cannot afford to be inattentive to a situation that affects not only the security of the oil supply but more importantly the very *validity* of its own nuclear deterrent.

20 August 1990

THE SQUARED HORIZON

How can we fail to recognize, after a month of standoff, that the true *intervention force* in the Gulf is television? And more precisely CNN, the Atlanta network. Saddam Hussein, and George Bush, certainly, but also Ted Turner, the owner of Cable News Network.

Henceforth, diplomacy is effective only through *interposed images*. To deploy, here or there, an invincible armada no longer has any meaning outside the express condition of strategically occupying the screen (live coverage), the image prevailing over that of which it is nevertheless only the image.

Once a way of weighing words, most often in saying nothing, the diplomatic exercise now involves weighing images in order to show nothing, or nearly so, in the manner of that unidentifiable flying object numbered F117 ... Today, for example, the President of the USA constantly watches CNN − one of the principal lines of communication, and faster than the regular diplomatic channels − to the point that even he was disturbed by Saddam Hussein's public provocations, and relied upon CNN to transmit various messages to the Iraqi people.

Is it still a matter of convincing public opinion? Certainly not. The live image advances no position, but only at the most an emotion, a certain apprehension: 'We pass from joy to despair in a few minutes,' explains a British hostage. *A hostage of the televisual interface*, the tele-spectator becomes directly involved in an uncertainty principle dependent upon the very rhythm of 'communiqués', in the manner of embassy officials.

The significance of these different 'messages' no longer resides in the *durée*[1] dedicated to the televised transmission, but primarily in the very long time span of the threat. In fact, this new 'televised series', which began on 2 August last year [1990], will probably not be completed until the end of the affair in the Gulf, in a month, a year, or longer − who knows?

21

To focus and concentrate the public's attention is progressively to reorganize the public's regime of temporality, its *use of time*, much more than public opinion. The live image is a filter, not through the space and the frame of the screen, but first through its time: a mono-chronical filter that does not allow *the present* to pass away. We are in the grips of a videoscopic technology that has nothing to do with film analysis or the critique of domestic television, a logistics of perception necessary for the progressive acquisition of the neural targets that we have become.

It is therefore useless to investigate what still distinguishes 'news' from 'propaganda'; the question is already no longer current, active – interactive – disinformation never being a lie, but rather the excess of contradictory news, hypernews [*surinformation*].

Everything is true in the offensive of direct broadcasting, 'true' in the instrumental sense of the term, that is to say, operationally and immediately efficacious. The audiovisual landscape becomes a 'landscape of war' and the screen a *squared horizon*, overexposed with video salvos, like the field of battle under the fire of missiles.

Much more than a *tele-audition* (Radio London during the German occupation, for example) or a *tele-vision* (CBS, ABC, NBC, etc., during the Vietnam War), it is now a matter of a *tele-action*, where the opposing parties are engaged in an *absolute interactive situation*, before the eyes of all, thanks to the broadcast transmissions of TV networks, CNN among others.

In this sudden war of real time, as in the real space of the Gulf, the means matter little – satellite, TV, missiles, tanks

– since all that matters is the end. The morality of the end justifies all the mediated or political means, but this *end* is no longer that of a conflict concerning this or that country; it is primarily *the end of the delay* [*délais*], the imperious necessity of an absolute proximity between civil and military protagonists, with the admitted objective of reducing to nothing the lapse of time between intentions and action.

Let us recall that once people fought *by day*, never by night. Also, one fought in the *summer*, never in the winter – and from this the 'ides of March' that inaugurated, in Rome, the season of hostilities. Today, heir to nuclear deterrence, war has become a total and ubiquitous phenomenon where image is one 'munition' among others. It matters little what thing (plane, tank, warship, etc.) is in question, nor does it matter what image is employed (radar, video, etc.); what matters is *their presentation in real time.*

Recently, at the demand of consumer groups, an anti-replay law was instituted in the USA, designed to suppress this practice, on the stage as on television. A sign of the times, war itself is no longer satisfied with the replay, it demands direct transmission.

With disinformation (*deception*), it is no longer a question of a *propaganda fide*, that is, the propagation of a certain 'faith' (in victory, for example), or even of an ideological or political conviction, but simply of a tact, of an impact, in other words a tele-action in the home.

Just as meteorological prediction is no longer merely an ordinary news item, so is tele-control, the tele-alarm of public opinion, not a propagandist practice (in the manner of Goebbels, for example) but, before all else, *the process*

23

of focusing a public image, the production of a certain *high-definition transmission* of collective reality.

What previously was played out over the course of a day in the newspapers, then in an hour on the radio, henceforth plays out in an instant, the real instant of the televised communiqué. Here is to be found the difference between the propagandistic use of contemporary cinema since the last world wars, and the use of global television in the Gulf crisis. What is 'globalized' initially is TV; it is not, or not yet, war. If the temporal régime of the news programmes of Fox-Movietone or Pathé-Journal was that of *deferred time*, analogous to that of the mainstream press, with the liberation of the media and the appearance of networks such as CNN, time dominates − that is, *real time*. A practical *durée* that permits no reflection, no critical distance, a time lapse that no longer distinguishes between the *before* or *after* − attack or defence − with the fatal risks of confusion that this entails.

Henceforth joined together, neither *for* nor *against* [*contre*] war or peace, but *right up close* [*tout contre*], in a conflict of proximity that is also a conflict of interpretation, since we no longer have the time needed to develop an opinion, instead only enough time to pass from one reflex to the next.

Blurred perception, adversaries suddenly unnaturally allied, yoked together by the media, linked remotely against their wishes by the screen, that apparent horizon of a stage on which no holds are barred: when is the *hour of truth* between Bush and Hussein?

Finally, the quintessential symbol of this conflict, the Stealth F117, a flying object that resembles a synthesized

24

image. Confirmation, if needed, that the image prevails over that of which it is the image, this machine was conceived in the 1980s in order that no equivalent radar signature could appear on the enemy's control screens.

There is a contradiction between the specifically aerodynamic requirements of a war plane and the *icodynamics* of its distant representation; the F117 represents a different sort of material. Slower, less manoeuvrable, no more equipped with armaments than the F15, F16 or F18, it represents nevertheless an unprecedented innovation in the duel of arms and armour, since the demand for its electromagnetic disappearance prevails over its destructive capabilities and even its mobility.

Continuing then: every type of military machine lies within two categories of the 'real', by virtue of the means of object acquisition: the *actual presentation* – the plane is there and it is identified optically and acoustically – and the *virtual representation* – the plane is not there, but it has sprung up on the radar console.

The designers of undetectable weapons must at all costs (and such is also the case with speech) eliminate the virtual representation so that the sole presentation is that of the moment of action, *the real time of the destructive act.*

To abolish the time of early tracking by cancelling the echo surface of radar waves, so that the unidentified flying object springs up like Death; thus, as in the example of the man who lost his reflection in the mirror, the F117 lost its electromagnetic image.

The nature of dissimulation is changing; planes are not so much camouflaged here as dissimulated elsewhere. The

25

strategic necessity of blurring the distant image prevails over camouflage, it gives its enigmatic form to the plane and allows its pilot to be there, *live*.

It is the prohibition of the replay. Since the invention of tele-detection, we would see a plane advancing before it was present; henceforth, we will not see it until it is already actually present, that is, *too late*.

With the Gulf Crisis, thanks to CNN-*live*, the converse is effected: we see the war *too early*, everything is already there, already seen and who knows, perhaps already played?

2 September 1990

THE WAR TO COME

Towards the end of the Vietnam conflict, the commanding general of the US Air Force asked, 'Why seven years, when seven seconds would have done it?'. Today, in the Near East, this question is raised anew, this question of the *durée* of a war in the making: 'Time is on Saddam Hussein's side,' it is said, or conversely, 'Much time is needed for the embargo to be effective.'

In fact, two regimes of temporality are imbricated in the space of the Iraqi–Saudi border: the long *durée* of a state of international siege and the excess celerity of the various means of communication and destruction arrayed.

The situation of the armed forces in this region of the world has nothing in common with the Vietnamese theatre of war. *The desert is a screen* where all is exposed to the searching eye of an adversary employing the full array of object-acquisition systems: advanced alert satellites, AWACS and aerial reconnaissance devices, piloted or automatic, such as the tele-commanded drones employed extensively by the Israelis in the region . . .

If, unfortunately, this conflict was bound to erupt, it would therefore be *overexposed*, not only in the eyes of the tele-spectators of the entire world but also in those of the military in both camps.

'It is the viewers who make the painting,' Marcel Duchamp told us yesterday. Tomorrow, and the day after tomorrow, it will be the tele-spectators who will make the war, the paintings of electronic battle! Meanwhile, in the basement of the Pentagon in Washington, the theatre [*salle*] of operations for this future *live show* has just been completed: C^3I, the official designation for Control, Command, Communication, Intelligence.

The screen becomes, therefore, the telescopic sight for a war where the attention of each is mobilized, whether he likes it or not. The horizon of the control monitor supplants both the military communiqué and the press, that mainstream press still necessary for analysis, for reflection.

Henceforth, whether we like it or not, the conditioned reflex will tend to prevail, and from this the serious risks of this year-end, but especially this *fin de siècle*.

Finally, let us consider in particular, from among the numerous estimates concerning the date of the unleashing of hostilities in the Near East, the 17th of November. Why this date? Precisely because on this day, not only will the American elections take place but especially because at this moment *we will enter a moonless period* that gives an offensive

27

advantage to the American forces equipped with night-vision capacity . . .

2 October 1990

THE EXERCISE OF LIMITS

'For he who has perfectly understood that he is mortal, the agony begins,' wrote Arthur Schnitzler at the end of the nineteenth century. What are we to say today, at the end of the millennium, of the fascination for certain extreme, if not suicidal, sporting activities, such as the base jump, which consists of throwing oneself, from a cliff, a bridge, or an apartment tower, only to open a parachute at the last possible moment? And what of the bungee jump, where the lover of vertigo experiments with free fall, placing his confidence in a bit of rubber?

Consider the words of one of these heroes, Bruno Gouvy, who died on 15 June last year, in the exercise of his 'art': 'It is, above all, an incredible sensual pleasure. The vision of the rockface upon which it seems you are about to be impaled, which then whizzes by, just a few metres away, is unreal. It is the strongest emotion, perfect bliss.'

If the tragic stage consists, since antiquity, in obviating death, these sports extremists are inaugurating an original tragedy whose sole spectator is generally a photographer, a cinematographer or journalist, witness to this death-defying challenge.

A risk-taker of the mediated era, the lover of the death jump realizes his feat only, in fact, in the *presence of his advo-*

28

cate; in other words, before the privileged 'mediator' who is capable of both recording his fall and confirming its interest through the eyes of the telespectators comfortably installed in their living rooms. *'If people pay attention to me, it's because I leave myself open,'* explains Thierry Donnard, director and producer of the film *Pushing the Limits*.

Thus, following the example of political extremism and terrorism, these suicidal sports need the media, need these screens where their feats leave their trace. Without the transmission of the image in the sensational press, the exercise of limits would make no sense, for, as Schnitzler also wrote, 'even suicide becomes absurd if it does not cause someone distress, it is nothing more than a flight into the void'.

The void that is at issue here is the sudden *fall in full view* of an individual in the crowd seen by others – no longer the stage of the theatre, arena or circus, but a televisual stage in the process of an accelerated globalization – whence this 'vertigo' of a new genre that becomes exhibitionist, the vertigo of both a jump into the void and a dive into the imaginary, the collective unconscious of a nonetheless solitary manifestation. An English psychiatrist from the 1970s, when speaking of our contemporaries, underlined the point that 'they do not want to die, they want to be dead'. This was, moreover, confirmed today by the French director of *Ushuaia*, a programme for the general public focusing on extreme sports, who stated, to those who wished to listen, that *'we need sometimes to feel as if we are between life and death'*.

In effect, these sporting practices can only proliferate, as is the case currently, by virtue of face-to-face coverage, the televisual exposition of two types of individualism: the first is adept at *cocooning* and the return to the home of play activities; and the other is accomplished in *sky surfing* and extreme sports. Without one, the other would not exist, socially speaking. It is the same with the terrorist who knows the time of televised news programmes and who plans the explosion of his bomb and the murder of innocents so that they will be aired on the evening news.

What is nevertheless serious is when these 'apostles' of extreme sports gain, as is the case today with the bungee jump, hundreds of emulators, to the point that we now speak, particularly in France, of the necessity of regulation to guarantee the 'reliability and safety' of this type of suicidal activity!

On 20 October last year, Gladis Guye, a 75-year-old retiree, accomplished a bungee jump of 85 metres from a cliff in the high country around Nice, under the eyes of her doctor, who was able to confirm a decline in his patient's tension following the jump. Soon this type of exercise will be *prescribed*, like those anti-depressant medications that so closely resemble intoxicants.

Oddly, since the expanse of the world is progressively being reduced to nothing, with the current employment of supersonic transports and instantaneous communications, the individual becomes his own training ground [*terrain d'exercice*], his own unique domain of exploration. Where the finite world starts, there begins the introspection of limited sensations, the practical exercise of an intensivity that resembles the nihilism of the past or the addiction to hallucinogens.

See how Laurent Bouquet, sky surfer, describes her fall from 4,000 metres up, surfboard on her feet, at nearly 200 kilometres per hour:

The speed of a free-falling body creates an incredible resistance. One has the impression of floating on a mattress of air, but by the time the fall has gone for 3,000 metres it is like tons. Even if in perfect physical condition, one would be killed instantly. Nevertheless, when I stopped for three months, I really missed it. My body has gone through its adrenaline withdrawal.

To simulate our own death, to become a bomb, to feel the call of the air of the tomb like a profound beatitude, what sort of perversion is this? If not to equal the *fall of angels* in a jump of one minute that lasts an eternity, as Bruno Gouvy demonstrates, the 'missile man' throws himself into the void of several thousand metres, his head and arms sunken into a warhead, attaining 539 kilometres per hour, the world record speed for a free fall, a feat carried out for the demand of a TV magazine.

These are just so many harbingers of a mutation in contemporary humanity's relationship to time. A 'time', a *durée of no duration* [*sans durée*], that only expresses itself [*s'exprime*] through that which it suppresses [*supprime*]. A future of a new regime of temporality of so-called 'advanced' societies where acceleration is fast becoming the common denominator of all industrial activities, economic or political, to the point of precluding the influence of time, of ageing or memory, solely to the end of forgetting or loss.

In the moment when we openly give up hope for our children, when we abandon millions of infants in Brazil and elsewhere, when will the 'moment of truth' be no longer only aesthetic but rather ethical? When will there be a return of a political intelligence of Time; when an end to this disastrous pollution of the temporal *durée* akin to that of the spatial extension [*étendue*]^2 of the World?

9 November 1990

THE SECOND FRONT

In 1897 M. I. S. Bloch wrote:

> As war has become a sort of pointless game in which no armies are able to get the upper hand, they will remain opposed, always threatening but incapable of striking a decisive blow. Consider the future: not combat but famine, not killing but the bankruptcy of nations for the ruin of every social system.

Less than a century after this prophecy we can thus observe, with little joy, the peripeteiae of the relationship between the East and West since the 'pointless game' of nuclear deterrence effectively ruined the two military super powers: the USA experiencing a bankruptcy of imagination with an administration in a state of temporary default, thirty-five million Americans living below the threshold of poverty and the increasing violence of urban crime that is a civil war in everything but name.

32

Indeed, despite agreements such as the 1975 Helsinki Accord, the great powers have so far proven incapable of checking the emergence of ever-new means of destruction. Thus the *era of deterrence* will have finally amounted to nothing more than the period in which the two opposing blocs instituted a series of automatisms, of industrial, scientific and economic procedures eliminating all political choice. In becoming 'strategic', it is the weapons themselves that deterred any interruption in the movement of the arms race, their production becoming predestined, this predestination of production of the means of destruction that, little by little, pulled the populace down, despite themselves, into a moral servitude without glory . . . Until the establishment of those computer-controlled 'engines of the last judgement', weapons of instantaneous communication, capable, through a *simple error of estimation*, of releasing a destructive force equal to that let loose during the entirety of the Second World War 'and this, in each second of the long afternoon that would be necessary for the launching of all the missiles, and all the bombs . . . *in each second a Second World War will have taken place*'.[3]

With this programming of the apocalypse momentarily suspended and with the signing of the disarmament agreements in Paris in November 1990, in the framework of the CSCE,[4] we can now only wonder what economic and social alternatives to this system of ruin are to be found.

Since the 1950s, men such as the physician and Nobel laureate Werner Heisenberg have attempted to answer this question. Heisenberg suffered no illusions and prophesied our entrance *into a state of permanent conflicts, of struggles*

33

aimed at mastering the influence made possible through a final state of global unification directly stemming from the nuclear status quo.

The current conflicts in the Middle East appear to be inaugurating this new era of disturbances in a particularly sensitive region (rich in petrodollars). Conflicts that later could well become among the most extensive in the world, first after the model of the *intifada* popularized by television, with the help of the 'lost children' of Muslim immigration, then with those of other ethnic or religious groups arriving in numbers from Africa, Asia or the countries of Eastern Europe, thus opening a *second front*, this one urban, that could eventually accomplish the destabilization of European democracies begun during the Cold War by an international terrorism itself largely dependent upon the media.

The post-Cold War period thus risks embroiling us in a global and total civil war, a 'Lebanonization' of the great cities that would prove to be only a perversion of the old 'anti-city strategy' of nuclear deterrence, thus nullifying the recent Paris agreements on the security of Europe.

Let us not forget, atomic weapons profoundly modified the political constitution of the great democracies, with this era of 'super-presidents' that gave a single man such exorbitant military power, disqualifying, in effect, the old parliamentarian representation. Entirely turned towards external politics and the international questions, these presidents, as Richard Nixon had already confirmed, were henceforth no longer indispensable to the internal life of the nation.

It will not be long before we see the result of this disengagement of political power. At the very time when we

34

were preoccupied with the *global expansion* of the great blocs, made possible by the new capacities of the means of communication, we were conversely facilitating on the ground a disquieting *contraction* in the field of human activities: a depopulating and progressive laying fallow of both rural and industrial areas, along with the great burnt-out suburbs where bit by bit all commerce is disappearing, every social interface ... in anticipation of an ultimate regression of a democracy that has become paradoxical, because of the de-urbanization of its sphere of election [*lieu d'élection*], the city.

Take, for example, Margaret Thatcher, who, since 1979, has known how to confront the most serious difficulties. She has been disavowed by her own party, notably because of her urban policies and the institution of a poll tax, that protectionist law aimed at driving out to the limits of the large cities a social margin now comprised of the masses. Hostile to the territorial unity of Europe, the Iron Lady hoped, in short, to replace the bygone British insularity with an *urban insularity* that would make cities such as London rich in ghettos where there would somehow survive a sort of English democracy of the 'select few'.

We can easily imagine the future of these utopian cities: after Belfast, Beirut has already shown us how the old communal city can collapse in on itself, with the reappearance of 'warlords' worthy of the Middle Ages, military employers of idle a-national gangs fighting without end for a neighbourhood, a street, or the ruins of a building.

In considering this tragic destruction of the convivial life of the Lebanese, we can only wonder whether, since by

35

1993 borders will no longer separate the European nations, they will, in time, reconstitute themselves, as in Beirut, in the very interior of the great cities.

The signs are multiplying before our eyes: the augural destruction of the Berlin Wall, the opening of borders and the gradual establishment of a liberal democracy in the East that, far from gathering the citizens together, or fostering in them the desire to reconstruct their country's economy, rather compels them to give up on everything and take off — these nations, if nothing is done, will undoubtedly lose between twenty and thirty million inhabitants in the years to come.

It is not a question, therefore, of immigrants dreaming of returning to their countries, their fortunes made, or of political refugees whose lives would be threatened by returning home, but rather that of a generalized desertion, of an ever-expanding army of proletarians in flight.

Having escaped the old law of the war between nations, will they become again like those hordes of whom Livy spoke at the beginning of our era: appearing and disappearing at the borders of regions, at the edges of rich ancient cities, 'thumbing their noses at war, exempt from the call to arms'?

The last confrontations and sackings of cities that occurred simultaneously in Berlin, London, Rome and Paris could lead us to believe as much. The conference on the definition of borders and migrations, planned for the end of January 1991 in Vienna, under the aegis of the Council of Europe, will therefore be exceptionally important.

3 December 1990

COUNTDOWN

The principle of the jet engine is simple: given a hermetically sealed cylinder, filled with a highly compressed gas, the pressure exerts itself against the walls. If one opens the back of the cylinder, the gas escapes and the pressure on this part of the wall disappears and ceases, eventually establishing an equilibrium of pressure that continues to exert itself against the front wall. Thus it pushes the cylinder in that direction, creating the propulsion. Once there is no further need of force for traction or for the propeller to propel the system, the *reaction is sufficient*.

The first to have the idea of employing this principle of propulsion to a vehicle was the automobile designer von Opel, who in 1928 created a car, and, ten years later, a jet glider. Meanwhile, in 1929, Fritz Lang and Thea von Harbou invented the first *countdown* in history, on the occasion of the launching of a missile over the beach at Horst, in Pomerania, for the purposes of the film *Une Femme sur la lune*[5] — an experimental missile designed by Hermann Oberth, pioneer in the conquest of space for the Nazi researchers.

4. 3. 2. 1. Fire! The result of this reverse course is always the same: immobility, the failure or explosion of a hasty departure. An *anti-chronological method* that owes everything, or nearly everything, to photographic instantaneity, to cinema, both to Fritz Lang and Georges Méliès, the inventor of special effects capable of *apparently re-editing time* [*remonter le temps*]. This hasty procedure does not today seem problematic, not even to philosophers. Nevertheless, the inversion of the unfolding of time is not a negligible matter, as it

paradoxically associates every *durée* with the reversibility of a palindrome and thus introduces into our everyday experience a practical reversion, to the point that no one is any longer surprised by this double reading of temporal reality. The process has attained a certain banality thanks not only to film projections but especially to television *replay*. The 'time machine' [*machine à remonter le temps*][6] is finally with us, transporting us back even to the astrophysics of the famous Big Bang, and leading us across the past millennia to the primordial explosion, the *countdown of the birth of time*!

At the beginning of the twentieth century, it was not enough that Alfred Wegener discovered continental drift, for Edwin Hubble also had to detect, again in 1929, the drift of galaxies, the universal expansion. From that point on, the involution of the space and time of generalized relativity was conceivable.

Note that the 'final solution' will not be limited, in this epoch, to the immediate extermination of Jews in hermetically sealed 'concentration camps', where gas played a role, not just for propulsion, but for the elimination of the living; it is also, and above all, a transgressive principle of extermination of the *durée*, *of the eternal return* to the zero degree of history, that remains to be analysed.

Flashback, the film is replayed in reverse, water flows up into the bottle, we walk backwards faster and faster . . . witnesses to demolitions see the destroyed building reconstructed, its walls returning to their places at the very top of the building. Regarding recent history, it is the inverse: the Berlin Wall is destroyed, the Soviet Union breaks up and Germany is abruptly reunified.

Once, the classical example of the palindrome was: *Esope reste ici et se repose*;[7] today, no one stays at rest, all is in flight and is displaced in a strange inverse transmigration. The habit of returning to our source, of rediscovering our origins, our 'identity', suddenly seems an absolute necessity. To accomplish the backwards journey, to become again what we were yesterday, the regression that leads back to the *point of departure* is like some parlour game.

Not long ago, a year or two, a courier on foot accompanying the Paris–Dakar rally completed the Ténéré Desert stage *walking backwards*, guided by a team-mate running at his side!

To be or not to be a tape recorder that we rewind, a film that we run backwards to the emergency stop, such is the question, the challenge of a generation with no future – *now future*.

Bringing us to the beginning of this new year. Not a leap year, but a palindrome – the numbers can be read either way, which is quite rare.

The countdown of the history of a threat also: August, September, October, November, December 1990 – 5. 4. 3. 2. 1. January 1991 . . . (the 15th to be exact) when we dare to speak again of the use of atomic weapons and not only for the limited role of deterrence we imposed upon them over the last forty years: 40, 30, 20, 10.

In short, the end of a period of grace, the 'endgame' of a period of our history where the geopolitics of the East and West blocs stabilized the sword of Damocles over the head of a world that was, yes, sick, but at least not in ruins.

Let us then assess the state of affairs: everything is in

place for the *first total electronic war of history*, a war of real time, of the microsecond and of impalpable waves of radiation or gas (still) — and also of tele-detection, since seven or eight KH11 spy and Lacrosse satellites are constantly surveying the movements of the opposing forces, while below them fourteen or fifteen AWACS and other surveillance planes control the aerial space and identify at 400 kilometres' distance flying objects, friend or foe. All these devices for the 'management of the battlefield' electronically transmit photos, films and coded messages directly to the Pentagon's computers in Washington. This data is relayed back to the land, sea and air intervention units in the Gulf in order to identify the strategic targets and the missions of engagement for the different weapons. This data is immediately transferred in a MIPSY and the cassette is then inserted into the computer that will guide the entirety of the mission, all within less than an hour.

How can we fail to realize finally that war is no longer 'the continuation of politics by other means' but only its failure? A failure that arises from the change in the nature of power, the change in its weapons of inordinate power that lack any relationship to the objective, the goals of war of the opposing states.

In Egypt, in the Temple of Karnak, the Dromos — the Avenue of the Sphinxes — leads visitors from the light of day to the darkness of the sanctuary of Amon, the solar idol of ancient Thebes. Where will the palindrome lead us tomorrow? To peace or the dreaded explosion?

Guess.

11 January 1991

III

January 1991: Desert Storm

J.-C. Raspiengeas: Despite its deadly nature, what are your views on the new television series entitled: *From the Invasion of Kuwait to the Gulf War*?

Paul Virilio: It illustrates perfectly Kipling's saying: 'The first victim of war is the truth.' Since 2 August we have been living in a theatre of operations, spectators of a theatrical production [*mise en scène*]. We have been living in a complete fiction. Faced with war, we must be not only conscientious objectors but also objectors to the objectivity of its representation. We must not believe our eyes. All is, if not rigged, at least arranged by one or several directors [*metteurs en scène*]. Saddam Hussein on one side, CNN on the other.

J.-C. R.: Which is the more skilful of the two?

P. V.: Ted Turner, the big boss of CNN. For ten years, he has been constructing the theatre of 'real time', of the live broadcast that causes us to take as true that which we see live. The Romanian affair should have served as a lesson.

J.-C. R.: This omnipresence of the media, of CNN in particular, has it changed the nature of the conflict?

P. V.: Completely. War henceforth takes place in a stadium, the squared horizon of the screen, presented to spectators in the bleachers. Now, the only way of existing is to participate in the passion of the game, to no longer be content to keep count of the goals scored between the international force allied with the United States and Iraq. I see guys fighting it out in the bleachers as at Heysel. Mimicking in their corner an *intifada* or whatever scene that the TV has presented on nightly news programmes.

J.-C. R.: Can it be said that the media have played a strategic role?

P. V.: Remember: we live in a communication society linked by electromagnetic waves that allow for direct broadcasting. The technologies offer a tele-presence to the entire world. With their placards written in English, the protestors of Tiananmen Square or Red Square present the demonstration to us. And we, sitting home, demonstrate with them.

Curiously, telecommunications put properties of the divine into play in civil society: the ubiquity (to be all present together at the same time), instantaneity, immediacy, omnivoyance, omnipresence. Each of us is metamorphosed into a divine being, at once here and there, at the same time. Whence our arrogance: I could say what I think about what is going to happen to a guy in six months or fifteen hours in the Arabian desert, although I know so little about him. It is totally absurd.

The place of politics in ancient societies was the public space (plaza, forum, agora . . .). Today, the public image prevails over the public space. Television has become the forum of all emotions and opinions. One votes while watching TV. War plays with this partnership and it is not by chance if the major states block the images.

We are heading towards a cathode democracy, but

without rules. Everything stands without support. It is a formidable situation.

J.-C. R.: How can we master this future game of images?

P. V.: Immediacy, ubiquity, omnivoyance are the elements of the politics of tomorrow. For the present, nobody controls real time. Nobody seriously poses the questions of its effects . . . All distances are reduced to zero. This global reduction will have fateful consequences for the social being, for morality. It is time to found an ecology of the media.

J.-C. R.: What is really threatened?

P. V.: The threat is that of fusion and confusion. No politics is possible at the scale of the speed of light. Politics depends upon having time for reflection. Today, we no longer have time to reflect, the things that we see have already happened. And it is necessary to react immediately. Is a real-time democracy possible? An authoritarian politics, yes. But what defines democracy is the sharing of power. When there is not time to share, what will be shared? Emotions.

A change in our relationship to time has recently taken place. Before, we had the past, the present and the future. Today, the choice is nothing more than that between deferred time and real time. Humanity no longer lives in the present, but rather in the tele-presence of the world. On the level of morality, of aesthetics, of ethics, major political questions immediately arise.

This change and this acceleration have modified the conduct of war. Ancient war depended upon the citizen-soldier. Progressively, with automated destruction and

43

nuclear weapons that impose a dramatically shortened period of decision, we have delegated the political power of the major states to a single man, the head of the state, who himself delegates the execution to a machine. Soon, war will be waged by automatic answering machines. The new weapons being designed will strike their objectives with a lightning speed of nanoseconds or milliseconds. At the speed of light, man can neither see the weapon arrive nor fend off the attack.

The Gulf War is the first total electronic war. Broadcast live, via satellite. The 'Star Wars' project already provoked from Gorbachev the following response to Reagan: 'If you continue, we will lose our final power of decision: to declare and manage war. Neither you nor I will be able to react to the attacks of the adversary. Our power will be in the hands of automated transmissions between satellites.' The *expert-systems* are the absolute *deus ex machina*.

J.-C. R.: How can this acceleration be checked?

P. V.: There is a certain inevitability in the domain of science and technology. We never decelerate. We could never again invent the slow train that took three weeks to go from Lyon to Paris. It's a problem of political philosophy: what does this idolatry of acceleration in the history of humanity since the night of time mean?

With the Gulf War we are literally living in weightlessness. Through public opinion we not only lecture the soldiers who burn in the heat of the desert and suffer, but judge them as well. A crazy situation, because it's false. In reality, we are all disarmed. Voyeurs and victims. In this prospective war there will be only victims. The capacities of destruction and of ecological disaster are such today that war is no longer a means but rather a drama. A major accident. The technologies employed are too powerful.

War was always linked to perceptual phenomena, such as I call the 'logistics of perception'. The technologies are such that it no longer suffices to camouflage a plane, but instead its path must be camouflaged to conceal its movements by means of disinformation (deception) that fabricates false random trajectories. The ruses of war are as old as war, except that today the deception is in images, radar signatures, electronic countermeasures.

J.-C. R.: The acme of the ruse of war is the American F117, this 'stealth plane' that you have described as 'resembling an image of synthesis'.

P. V.: This plane has two constraints: aerodynamics and icodynamics. Its form is linked not only to the requirements of movement in space but also to the requirements of its remote representation. It's extraordinary! That the remote image of an object should have an effect on the object itself is a very important event in the history of the image. And philosophically, it's vertiginous.

J.-C. R.: Has the image become a weapon like the others?

P. V.: In any case, a munition that causes a lot of trouble. As a weapon, it is first of all an eye that takes aim. No murders without aim. Meanwhile, cameras are incorporated in missiles to guide them to the target. And beyond that, with satellites the entire world is under tele-surveillance.

J.-C. R.: Who is behind Big Brother?

P. V.: Ted Turner again. It is he who operates the great global video production. He is a partner in the events. How is he going to circumvent military censorship? It is going to be particularly interesting to see the change in CNN during the war.

J.-C. R.: A few months ago you wrote, 'In the Gulf Crisis, thanks to CNN, we see war too early, everything is already there, already seen, and who knows, already played.' What would you like to say?

P. V.: The essence of a stealth warplane is that we see it too late, it is already there. We did not have time to prepare ourselves to see it. It is the same thing with the technology of the real time of CNN.

We do not have time to prepare ourselves for an event, it has already taken place. We are summoned to accept it or refuse it. Live television is a veritable injunction. One does not discuss a live image, one undergoes it.

A talk recorded 14 January 1991

WAR IN REAL TIME

Heraclitus wrote, 'It is necessary to extinguish excess[1] before the fire.' Since the night of 17 January, we have entered into the excess of a new war: the war of real time, of omnivoyance, and of omnipresence, that supplants the ground war, the war of real space that made up the history of nations.

First total electronic war, the current conflict in the Gulf no longer plays out only on the line of the front of a given geographic horizon, but first of all on the monitors, the control screens of televisions of the entire world. The perspective from the battlefield is no longer so much that of the point of departure as the simultaneous departure of all points, the pixels of the image of targets to be acquired in order to destroy the enemy.

With satellite ubiquity and the instantaneity of military telecommunication, this overexposed war assumes the traditional attributes of the divine, so much so that on one side is the *mystical* fundamentalism and Saddam Hussein's calls for a holy war, while on the side of the allies, we see a sort of *technical* fundamentalism, a call to pure war, with the support of sophisticated *matériel* (cruise missiles, smart bombs, etc.) that allows confrontation with the enemy almost without touching, *as if by nothing less than a miracle*, with the electromagnetic environment above the Iraqi territory effectively substituting for the normal milieu, the sphere of armed men.

Even if the coalition ground forces were soon to enter into action to liberate Kuwait, the most important aspect of this first week of fighting will have been marked by the extensive use of those 'weapons of communication' that will assure, along with weapons of mass destruction, the new military supremacy – it being understood that the means of mass telecommunication are included in this panoply, CNN having assumed on its own, or nearly, the bulk of the task.

Therefore, while the Vietnam War saw television *in deferred time* act almost exclusively on American public opinion (and we know the results), the Atlanta network *in real time* establishes the interaction of all peoples, as well as the public opinion of the entire world, with the obvious risk of producing an analogous effect on the opinion of these tele-spectators if the conflict in the Gulf is prolonged. They will find themselves brought together like 'fans' in the seats of a stadium, reacting to the feats of their favourite team. Let us hope that this stadium is not like that of Heysel and that this event does not trigger a second sort of conflict, this one civil, in Europe or elsewhere.

We are entering a *third era of war*. The end of East–West nuclear deterrence, with its strategic uncertainties, will result in the necessity of reinterpreting the doctrines of martial confrontation since the most distant origins of history.

If, according to Michelet, every epoch dreams the next, each historical conflict tends to imagine the next. We saw this with the First and Second World Wars, opening on to the era of atomic deterrence, and we will see it tomorrow with the 'disequilibrium of terror' and the premises of nuclear proliferation, the sketch of a deterrence of the 'strong by the weak' presaged by the Gulf Conflict.

If there are indeed three major epochs of war – the prehistorical *tactical* epoch, composed of restricted conflicts, then the historical and properly political *strategic* epoch and finally, the contemporary *logistical* era, where science and industry play a defining role in the destructive capacities of opposing forces – there are also three great types of weapons that follow in sequence of importance through the course of the ages: weapons of *obstruction* (ramparts, fortifications, armour), weapons of *destruction* (bows, cannons, missiles, etc.) and finally, weapons of *communication* (lookout and signal towers, various vectors, radio, radar, satellites, among others). With each of these 'weapons' there predominated a type of confrontation: the war of siege for the first, the war of movement for the second and total war, blitzkrieg [*guerre éclaire*[2]], for the last.

This era, in which military-industrial and scientific logistics prevail over the doctrines of use and over purely political arguments – war being no longer, according to Gorbachev himself, the continuation of politics by other means – opens on an epoch when the *weapons of instantaneous communication* are going to dominate, thanks to the development of a globalized news network and a generalized tele-surveillance.

A crucial question is therefore posed to those in political power: if the early warning satellites have created the impossibility of a surprise attack on Europe and have thus contributed to the disarmament under way between the military blocs, abolishing, in effect, *the deterrence of the strong by the strong*, of what type of interdiction will these 'weapons of communication' be capable when faced with the threat of atomic and chemical proliferation? As President Mitterrand explained not long ago:

Nuclear proliferation is not only a problem with regard to Iraq, it has to do with the safety of the world. At the risk of shocking them, I said to the Americans that an international conference was necessary to check the dissemination of nuclear weapons; if not, all will escalate.[3]

The first post-war conferences must therefore be dedicated

not only to Palestines and Lebanons but also to the sort of world that is seriously threatened by the 'disequilibrium of terror'. Whatever it may be, let us be clear again that it is not only bombs that are guided by television but so also especially public opinion; and in this 'war of real time', journalists are in the front line to win or lose, not the war, but the post-war, irrespective of what comes of the conflict in the Gulf.

19 January 1991

A MAJOR HISTORICAL ACCIDENT

A war that has just begun is like an infant that has just been born: no one knows its destiny. Thus, every war is new and extends what was until then unprecedented, that which has been neither spoken nor thought.

It is useless therefore, in the first days of combat, to enter into strategic or political predictions soon to be outdated by the very atrocity of the deadly action. The Gulf War does not escape this rule. Opening with the air offensive and its spectacular display, with which we are familiar thanks to *live* television, it will soon expand beyond the duel of Scud and Patriot missiles, through an attack of coalition ground forces, advancing into Kuwaiti and Iraqi territory.

As for the state of public opinion in the opposing countries, this depends in large measure on the number of casualties and the more or less fierce character of the opposing enemies. Whatever it may be, the political result will achieve less through ground combat, the real space of the Gulf War, than through the impact of the 'means of mass

50

communication' that extend the impact of the struggle between the Iraqis and the allies, and this, for the first time in the history of the media, *in real time*.

Even if the coalition forces use a surfeit of smart bombs, Tomahawk cruise missiles or the anti-missile Patriot missile, even if Saddam Hussein does not deny himself the use of his most sophisticated panoply of weapons, the novelty of this 'post-modern' conflict is essentially that of the satellites, both spy satellites and telecommunication satellites – let us not forget that on the very first night of hostilities, in Kourou, an Ariane rocket launched two broadcasting satellites, one Italian, the other European. What will not change, however, even if the rest is rapidly modified, is the presentation to the entire world of the effects of these murderous attacks, of this war that is 'worldwide', less in the expanse of the front than through the instantaneous retransmission in homes around the world.

As the Israelis put it not long ago, 'It's the first time that there has been a war in the Near East and that we are watching in bed, on TV.' The strikes of the first Scud on Tel Aviv did not change this fact, except that it would henceforth prove wiser to go down into the shelters to watch the course of operations . . .

It is therefore useless to try to estimate the degree of censorship, or the obvious absence of certain images from the front, with this *war in real time*; the most important issue is the impact, the very immediacy of the televised news. What video crews call 'image capacity' has nothing to do with 'high definition'. The important thing, as in a publicity clip, is to affect people's minds, to tele-affect

51

emotionally the tele-spectators before their screens. Space and the informative content of the image count infinitely less than time, the reality of a scene that plays out *live*, or with a slight delay. Finally, in this mediated strategy, journalists are all 'mobilized' and it is they, do not doubt it, who win or lose, not *war*, but the *post-war*, whatever may be the result of the conflict between the armed forces.

Since the development of nuclear deterrence, the Clausewitzian form is obsolete: mass war is no longer the continuation of politics by other means, *it is a major historical accident.*

Indeed, the very excess of the means employed in the conflicts engages the great powers — at once means of mass destruction and means of mass communication — leading to uncontrollable results, *politically speaking.* Even if the purely military outcome of the Gulf War can be envisioned, its political consequences are incalculable, as is the case also with the echo of global public opinion concerning this conflagration in the Near East.

No expert, no news specialist, can estimate the effects induced by 'war at home', and the example of Vietnam is not a good test case, since its effect depended solely upon televised news programmes in deferred time. The first total electronic war in real time will lead therefore to unforeseen and negative consequences that no one can apprehend today.

Up to this point, the military-industrial development of these 'miracle weapons' has been justified to the people by the necessity of deterrence, that is to say, on the basis of the non-use of the weapons, the Cold War arsenal being, supposedly, a guarantee of peace, an equilibrium of terror for Europe and the world. The actual use by Iraq and then

by the allies of this terrorizing material can only produce a
serious shock upon people's conscience, especially if this
use is contemplated *without the reflection* of some sort of
analysis of the losses.

Disciples of a true 'deterrence culture' for some generations now, Europeans, among others, will find it difficult to
be in the terror of a real war, legitimate or not. Those who
have up to now been 'sanctuaried', in other words,
protected and habituated to the scenarios of a perpetually
deferred apocalypse, will now be forced to contemplate the
fatal and bloody reality of all sorts of destruction.

We should be fearful that in addition to the excesses of
mystical fundamentalism and Saddam Hussein's call for a holy
war, Western tele-spectators will suddenly reveal themselves to be disciples of a *technical* fundamentalism and hear
the news from the front as a call to pure war against the
underdeveloped miscreants.

Note, meanwhile, that the orbital weapons currently in
play possess traditional attributes of the divine: omnivoyance
and omnipresence.

A true *deus ex machina*, the electronic war machine is not
neutral; politically, it represents a serious danger of contam-
ination of conscience for men of goodwill.

22 January 1991

TARGET ACQUISITION

The function of the weapon is first of all the function of the
eye: sighting. Before attaining his target, a hunter or a

warrior must always take aim, to align his target between the eyepiece and the sight of his weapon, exactly as a cameraman frames the subject that he is about to shoot. 'Silence, action' [*Silence, on tourne*] is therefore not far removed from 'Silence, fire' [*Silence, on tire*].

Missile-video or bomb guided by an installed camera, the new weapons are not appreciably different from those weapons of the past that also required a designation of the target by lit rockets or projectors.

Today, however, the difference is *indirect sighting*, the TV sighting that no longer works with the naked eye, but with electromagnetic waves at the very speed of light. Somewhat as in the cockpits of attack planes divided in two parts: the 'head-up' display (through the windscreen) and the 'head-down' display (on the control monitors on the console), 'post-modern' war requires a split observation, an immediate perception (with one's own eyes) and a mediated perception (video or radar). A kind of fleeting intoxication, an equivocation of perception,[4] the optic of the conflict is therefore above all an electro-optic in real time. We must keep this in mind when we interrogate, to put it aptly, the treatment of information by certain televisual media (CNN among others) on the subject of the Gulf War.

If every war requires its ruses, its lies of every sort, and therefore the necessity to be on guard, a new element now intervenes: while it was previously necessary to *dissimulate the object*, to camouflage it with 'war paint' or to conceal combat vehicles or firing positions from direct view, dappled and sheltered by camouflage nets, it is also now necessary to *camouflage the trajectories*, to direct the enemy's

attention away from the true trajectory to lure his surveillance towards false movements, towards illusory trajectories, thanks to decoys, electronic countermeasures that
'seduce' but do not 'requite' their weaponry.

To the doubling of vision already mentioned is soon to be
added a doubling of the trajectories of military objects
(planes or missiles): the *real trajectory* in the space of the
field of battle and the *virtual trajectory* in the electromagnetic
environment of these decoys, these countermeasures that
represent so many illusions for the adversaries. Thus, as was
announced a few years ago by Admiral Gorchkov: '*The victor
of the next war will be he who knows how to exploit the milieu of
the electromagnetic spectrum.*'

All of this, we note, with the certain advantage of the
speed these waves, propagated at the absolute speed of light,
have over the *matériel* of war that only moves at the relative
speed of some hundreds or thousands of kilometres per
hour. In this sense, the video or missile images, or the radar
signatures of their trajectory on the control screen of the
launching equipment (those of the Patriot anti-missiles, for
example), become true *iconic munitions* that allow for the
most rapid destruction of the enemy's devices (the Scud
missile launched by Iraq).

We note, therefore, that the war of images is no longer a
metaphor and that – as is the case with speech – it has
nothing to do with the images of war disseminated in
deferred time by the press. On the other hand, ever since
these military spots have been broadcast, disseminated in
real time, to the public of the opposed forces, iconic war
extends its destruction to the mind of each, with the incal-

55

culable political risks that this presupposes. Originally from Mondovi, Albert Camus wrote in effect on the subject of the Algerian War: 'If someone threatens my mother, I can no longer say anything.' Imagine now that one assassinates her *live, before his very eyes!*

Just as there is a doubling of the military optic on the theatre of operations, between the optic of real space of the vision of actors, and the electro-optic of the real time of military or civil tele-spectators, there is simultaneously a sudden *doubling of the front*, a commutation between the place of action – the Near East – and the place of its immediate reception – the entire world.

To the topical character of the air or land battle is added, therefore, the *tele-topical* character of the confrontation of different mediators. It is no longer a matter, as previously, of a tele-audition (the Second World War) or of a tele-vision (the Vietnam War), but indeed of a true tele-action, that is to say, the establishing of the interactivity of the partners in war: those actually making war, and those watching it *at the same time as their counterparts.*

It is therefore useless to speculate any longer on the nonexistent or nearly nonexistent informative content of the *live* images, or on the corruption occasioned by the CNN monopoly, for the essence is elsewhere. Like the publicity spot, the military spot is no longer exactly an 'image', but rather *a signal*, a video signal. Its space, its framing, is less important than its suddenness, and in particular less important than the way in which the news breaks upon public opinion, the experience of those who undergo it.

When all is said and done, the time of the *live* image

nullifies the space of its representation, to the exclusive advantage of an *untimely presentation* [*présentation intempestive*], lacking any rapport with usual information, since it is a matter only of a TV shot in which the power is to be found not in the content, the meaning, but solely in the rapidity of its delivery, in its immediacy.

Hyper-mediated, the military spots, of which we are the unconscious victims, are analogous to those *hypersonic* vectors that nullify all distance to the advantage of a pure arrival.

Just as the perspective of the event in real time in the *square* of the screen is no longer the perspective of the real space of the *line* of the horizon, so also the moment of *live* reception, '*the real moment*', is no longer the present moment, that of everyday experience, but a moment falsified by immediacy itself. As a result, with the *tele-present moment*, it is not necessarily the news that is false or subject to caution, but the lapse of time of its reception. As the theologian Dietrich Bonhoeffer wrote prophetically during the course of the Second World War: *Immediacy is an illusion.*

Today, war is no longer so much a war of 'images', but one of waves, war at the speed of light (take laser weapons, for example), this indirect light that illuminates and blinds the minds of a dumbfounded public, a light that will have been operated primarily by CNN, a *deus ex machina* that illuminates global public opinion.

Shortly before the Watergate affair, President Richard Nixon proposed the institution in the USA of an electronic process allowing the television sets of all American citizens

57

to be turned on remotely, *by executive order*, for direct alerts. With Ted Turner and his network CNN, it is no longer a matter only of alerting the USA but the world, the citizens of the entire world.

A dramatic accident of the circulation of information, the treatment in real time of the Gulf War by the media is the extension by other means of the *accident of deterrence*, such as is expressed in this conflict.

A major historical catastrophe, the Iraq–UN war is escaping, bit by bit, the military actions of the two camps, precisely by virtue of its uncontrollable psychological impact on a public who are undergoing, *eo ipso*, a major transformation, especially in Europe and the Mediterranean basin.

Even if the will to power of a dictator must be stopped as quickly as possible before the post-Cold War situation degenerates, the indirect consequences of this military operation cannot be neglected for long, under the pretext of providing total coverage – *live coverage* – of the event. How much longer will tele-spectators accept being informed, hour by hour, by newscasters, 'civilian' journalists acting as ongoing stand-ins for generals or admirals?

Let us not forget the declaration of that old journalist, Georges Clemenceau, who became a political figure during the First World War: 'War is a thing too serious to trust to the military . . .' I would add: the war of real time more than any other.

27 January 1991

58

FALSE MOVEMENTS

A friend living in Eastern Europe wrote to me recently:

Although the situation has changed in Romania during the last year, in a certain sense nothing has fundamentally changed. The battle for autonomy and against censorship of television continues. Mihaela Cristea, who was managing TV studios during the revolution, for example, finds himself in a difficult situation due to the political chaos. *The controversies concerning the subject of television have outlasted the revolution itself!*

The crises of the media were more important than those of the political. For how can we control a revolution when we ignore, fundamentally, where and when it really began? Maybe on 22 December 1989, when the local people occupied Romanian television during demonstrations, or even, at the other pole, nine months earlier, when, thanks to Western cameras, an uprising in a communist régime played out, for the first time in real time, before the eyes of the entire world?

How can we fail to recognize that for every major historical change, for each stage of the course of our history, there is a corresponding 'seizing of power' [*prise de pouvoir*] of a new technology of communication? We can hardly conceive of the rise of the Renaissance without the printing press, with the publishing, in a few lustra,[5] of millions of books. The century of the Enlightenment would perhaps not have happened without the powerful contribution of secret newspapers, and the French Revolution without the entirely

59

novel liberty accorded to the daily newspaper. Closer to us, the wireless telegraph and the Belinograph[6] gave rise to newspapers like the *New York Times*, which, with its own receiving station for transatlantic communications, *was the greatest news machine* at the beginning of the century.

After 1914, the popularization of cinematography meta-morphosed the old public discourse of the written press into mass vision, the *mass observation* that inevitably made a significant contribution to the tragic founding of totalitarian régimes in Russia, Germany and elsewhere. Radio broadcasting made possible an internationalization of the Second World War that could hardly have been realized without the technological means of information on the scale of the modern world: 12 March 1938, the day after the invasion of Austria by Hitler and the creation of the Anschluss, the first *multiplex[7] news transmission in history* passed over the waves. Thanks to the efforts of CBS, American journalists and correspondents could exchange their impressions and news directly, between London, Berlin, Vienna, Paris and Rome. In time, during the crucial years of the war, networks like NBC became involved in intense broadcasting, as the hunger for direct news could hardly be satisfied.

The real breakthrough of television in the USA took place in 1948, the same year that marked the beginning of the Cold War promoted by President Harry S. Truman, he who executed the first atomic attack in history. Later, television would become the ideal instrument of communication for a new epoch more transpolitical than political, an epoch of a *civil deterrence* destined to bring about the inertia of *nuclear deterrence*.

But already in 1962, in founding the CSC (Communications Satellite Corporation) to assure the cohesion of the American efforts, Congress foresaw the end of this mediated era. The successful launching of the satellite Telstar by American Telephone and Telegraph provided for the first live televised transmission between the USA and Europe and, in 1964, the attempt by Howard Hughes to launch a geo-synchronous satellite was a success. Four satellites of the same type, spread out over equal distances around the planet, would soon secure televised transmissions in all the inhabited regions of the globe.

In 1980, amid general scepticism, the mysterious Ted Turner founded CNN. Having satisfied the need for news and images, twenty-four hours a day, first only for Americans, he expanded the capacity of his network to reach the entire planet by renting a channel on five different satellites. CNN today serves ninety-one nations in both the East and West.

In fact, this *orbital tele-surveillance*, omnipresent and omnivoyant, strikes an undoubtedly fatal blow to national television networks, with their traditional programming at fixed times and in fixed places. It will not be long before CNN demonstrates the all-powerful nature of its transnational system by becoming the interlocutor chosen by the two opposed camps in the first hours of the Gulf Crisis.

Ever faster the global switchboard in real time; ever less informative, with military censorship soon to be imposed on the pool of journalists.

During the 1960s, the rock singer Mick Jagger said, 'The Rolling Stones draw their energy from chaos.' With

its fusion/confusion of distances and appearances, the televisual era that is upon us draws its energy from the creation
of a chaos, the first condition of the future escape from the
old global order. And from this comes the progressive
disavowal of existing institutions — political, labour, religious, familial — to the benefit of the unfolding on TV
screens of militant sub-groups being rapidly rendered obsolete. The extreme left in Japan, in one of the most
mediated countries in the world, was one of the first to go
to their street demonstrations equipped with cameras and
tape recorders, with the intention of recording their own
actions, the relay having been quickly taken up, however,
by an urban tele-surveillance that was in this instance no
longer incidental, but rather had an impact in real time on
the comings and goings of each and every person, as in
Tiananmen Square, where this technology played a significant role in the identification of demonstrators by the
Beijing authorities. During the 1960s, there were also the
large international gatherings such as Woodstock and the
cycloramas of the large stadiums where thousands of actor-
spectators crammed together, the cameras and the lasers
illuminating not only the rock stars but also the crowd and
its paroxysms. Pacifist groups, ecological groups, leftist
students, homosexuals, women's libbers, anti-racists, all
sorts of militants created, one after the next, 'their
cinema' in the arteries of the great metropolises with their
costumes, their more or less violent rites, their slogans
and their placards — often composed in the English
language — narcissistic demonstrations destined to establish
a sort of tele-active play with the cameras, linking up with

a television that had just become globalized . . . and this up to the perfectly programmed apotheosis of the destruction of the Berlin Wall, soon followed, right there, by several famous rock concerts.

Interdit d'interdire![8] ('Down with authority!') proclaimed a slogan of the 1960s. A transgression of the old normative regulations, subjugation to this new law would consist in denying all law. A vaguely Freudian scenario that fallaciously compares moral obstacles to material obstacles: we must level every obstacle, there must be no longer any obstacles to the immediacy of desire. An approach to liberation that would assure that we would no longer have to dare to act in the moment, for action would be made so easy that it no longer existed . . . If action is indeed a movement adapted to an end, a manifestation of the peculiarly human will, these approaches and 'false movements' would end, paradoxically, in the abolition of the individual will, and therefore of liberty itself.

Like those in the countries of the East who were trained to forgo the habit of expressing themselves in the first-person singular, or even those in the military overwhelmed by their demobilization at the end of a conflict: 'In the army, they told me what I had to do; now I must figure it out myself!'

Less permissive than dissuasive,[9] the era just past thus created, in the few generations of the Cold War and without anyone being particularly concerned, a generalized idleness, where unemployment is ultimately only one of the atrocious features.

2 February 1991

63

THE CRUISE OF THE MISSILE

The first image of this war: the foredeck of the battleship *Wisconsin*, the morning of 17 January, with dozens of crew members filming the departure of Tomahawk cruise missiles towards Iraq. The last, on 1 February: a sequence on Iraqi television showing the passage at low altitude of one of these cruising missiles, somewhere above Iraqi territory . . .

Why this memory? Because the murderous machine is a *robot*, a 'machine-transfer' from industrial war to post-industrial war, and also because it concerns a forerunner of the current *vision machine*.

In fact, the significant thing about this long-range munition is its electronic memory, a sophisticated device that houses the inertial guidance system that attains its distant objective. Initially directed by simple radar bearings of the territory overflown, the cruise missile came progressively to have a sophisticated topographic perception, to the point where the development of the automation of perception in the civil domain will prove to have been linked, twenty years later, to the constant improvement of the vision of these types of missiles.

Another aspect of the technological development of this aerial torpedo: it required a very probing, cadastral approach for most of the cities of Europe, and elsewhere required an exact census to inform the memory of the missiles about the construction of buildings and high towers in this or that region that could pose obstacles. During a certain period, in the Warsaw Pact countries and even the Soviet Union, we saw scaffolding towers constructed around

64

strategic sites in the probable paths of these missiles, not unlike the obstacles of fixed balloons used for anti-aircraft defence during the Second World War.

In order to avoid this type of problem for the cruise missile, it was quickly decided to provide it with *an indiscriminate vision*, with an electro-optic vision machine, to allow it to bypass these defences or avoid buildings recently constructed and not listed by the spy satellites.

Let us recall also another important element for the research and development of these projectiles: legally, *a missile is barred from violating any nation's air space* in the same way as is a piloted device (consider, currently, the problem of reprisals by Israel).

But let us return to the first image, to the deck of the *Wisconsin*, covered by sailors visibly enthused by the launching of the robots, applauding and photographing the flight of the automatons. This is not yet 'the war of the worlds', but it already resembles it. How can one actually rejoice at the automatism of a weapon called 'intelligent' without discrediting not only the enemy but equally the ally, the American soldier or another? Remember that these weapons were designed not for making war, the great mass war, but to prevent this for ever – that is, in the major states. The image of their launch in numbers in the Gulf War can only be interpreted as a serious failure of deterrence and of its military-industrial system of weapons production.

The Tomahawk taking off from the deck of the battleship at the beginning of this year *is a robot that frees itself*, that liberates itself suddenly from its tutelage. That was the first, anticipating the Patriot anti-missile missile a few days later, and above all anticipating the use of 'non-conventional' weapons also fully automated.

We can more accurately assess, now, the tragic significance of this 'strategic accident' that arose from the failure of a deterrence that was supposed to have been guaranteed by these weapons systems. Not only must the electronic memory of cruise missiles be entirely reprogrammed in order to correspond to the Near Eastern theatre of operations (as opposed to that of Europe and the East), but it is the military intelligence of the strategy of deterrence that must today be totally rethought, with the risks of the *disequilibrium of terror* that this implies.

When we see Dan Rather, the celebrity newscaster of CBS, returning twice during the 7 o'clock news to the image of the cruise missile sailing off towards its Iraqi objective, when this weapon was initially programmed to strike Dresden, Leipzig or Leningrad, we can legitimately ask where this sudden deprogramming of the post-industrial war machine will lead us.

The message of this *mediated* war is not therefore so much that of the news concerning the reality of present-day battles as that of the promotion of the virtuality of wars to come. War of the radically unthinkable, where the role of people in war would be only that of impotent tele-spectators and victims of 'intelligent' weapons that eliminate purely and simply 'unintelligent' weapons and the people who serve them. We can, meanwhile, legitimately wonder what will remain to be put on show, this year, in the salon of Bourget,[10] after the cathodic exhibition of all this material of war? *Why not the wreckage*, the ruins and the debris, the infirmity of a failed idea of deterrence? After all, this would not be the first time that one had attempted to excuse oneself to those one had hoped to protect.

2 February 1991

THE FOURTH FRONT

Since the beginning of the century, the news has constituted a fourth front. Next to the other three — earth, sea and air — *the news front* increasingly represents the most important in inter-state confrontations, nuclear deterrence having imposed upon adversaries, for more than forty years, a primary type of mutual reconnaissance, thanks to the plethora of spy satellites.

Nevertheless, as with public opinion and the great means of mass communication, there are, in the strategic domain, three principal movements for this type of confrontation where the arms are those of data, of figures, of images or of sounds: first, *insufficient information* [*sous-information*] or limited censorship; second, *the total absence of information*, a generalized censorship that some have called the 'weapon of silence', and which the Soviets exploited for years; and third, *disinformation by excess information* [*surinformation*], jamming, a saturation of meaning that the English call 'deception' and the Soviets *glasnost*.

Literally, this means an asphyxiation of the adversary's organs of analysis and interpretation by an increased unveiling of means, of methods and of secondary objectives, amounting to the establishment of the greatest confusion

possible – in fact, the same as that caused by the multipli-
city of the weapons systems in use today, where *the tactics of
saturation* are imposed upon the earth, sea and air.

Admiral Le Pichon declared on the subject of the first
crisis in the Gulf, during the period of the Iran–Iraq war:

> I would like to offer some reflections that have been an
> inspiration for me during the many hours I spent on the
> *Clemenceau* avoiding the traps of a confusing situation
> where errors were the norm. War, such as it is, is a
> source of infinite errors. In the case of the crisis in the
> Mediterranean as in the Gulf, where the confusion was
> enormous, *it is critical to be able to make an identification.*
> (*Libération*, 22 September 1988).

This gigantic confusion of minds, the fruit of the saturation,
electronic or otherwise, of the field of real battle, is
nothing, however, in comparison with that of the virtual
war to which the allies henceforth consign themselves in the
great game of the mediated war. To *make an identification*, to
interpret as quickly as possible the signs, images and trajectories, becomes thus the key phrase of this logistic of
perception that determines not only the nature of the war
but especially that of the post-war.

Henceforth, the fourth front becomes the principal front
and comes to supplement, indeed supplant, the strategies of
land, sea and air actions. After the necessary mastering of
air and orbital space, the question presents itself of the political and strategic mastering of time, of the real time of
simultaneous exchanges between nations and their threa-

tened populations. As Eduard Shevardnadze indicated to the
UN two years ago: 'War is no longer a rational instrument
of politics. *The end of secrecy becomes a security factor.*' In other
words, immediate information becomes the *ultima ratio* of
nations, excess information [*surinformation*] deters the rough
deterrence of bombs, tanks or missiles. We saw what
follows a year later, with the collapse of the Berlin Wall
and the decline of the Warsaw Pact.

Let us take note now of the situation of the press and
audiovisual media in the Gulf War: what is, for example, the
rule of conduct of the journalists and correspondents of
CNN, the first to have played a role in this conflict: '*The
facts, nothing but the facts!*' What arrogance, or rather what
self-importance. For even if there is a 'recoil-less weapon',
is there then a televised press, news without recoil, with no
critical distance? Certainly not. Televised or written – live
or delayed – any self-respecting news source always needs
time to reflect, that is, needs at least some minimal delay to
verify sources, a delay that no longer exists with *live* transmissions. Nearly forty years ago, Louis-Ferdinand Céline
wrote prophetically: 'For the time being only the facts count
and even this for not much longer.' Time is henceforth
obsolete, and the facts [*faits*] are fractured [*défaits*] by the very
immediacy of their electromagnetic transmission. Hence the
strategic importance for the Pentagon of the famous American 'pool reports' and the parsimonious opening of the pool
to other journalists of the coalition forces.

Faced with this situation, 'conscientious objection' is *de
rigueur*. It is thus absolutely necessary that neither journalists
nor tele-spectators *believe their eyes*, lest we allow ourselves,

69

sooner or later, to be fooled, as was the case last year in Romania.

The 'electronic battlefield' does not stop at the Iraqi–Saudi border; it now extends, through the mediation of satellites, to the entire world, to the global space of a planet threatened by who knows what mania: the conquest mania of a dictator, or the mania of a technology, of a science without conscience of which we must now be most wary.

The ethical principles of the international press, codified in the age of carrier pigeons or the transatlantic cable – in other words, in the era of the *deferred time* of mass information – must now most urgently be adapted to the era of *real time*. Otherwise, the Gulf War will usher in an unprecedented confusion in the media. Meanwhile, has not Ted Turner, the head of CNN, just asked children no longer to watch CNN? But now, whatever one says, whatever one shows, in the age of generalized interactivity, *it is dangerous to lean out of the window*.

6 February 1991

THE UNIFORM OR THE SUIT?

Bless my heart with a monotonous languor . . . The radio theme of the D-Day landings, 6 June 1944, comes to mind at the beginning of what will probably be a crucial week for the combatants in the Iraqi–Saudi desert.

How not to die? How to escape wounds, and the pain of body against body, if not by the ultimate and laughable

70

parade:[11] the helmet, the bullet-proof vest or armour? How to avoid the metallic impact, but especially the infiltration of toxic compounds, the gas? The choice of the military wardrobe is clear: the helmet and the uniform, the camouflaged combat uniform designed to be recognizable if possible between friends, allies, all the while passing unperceived before the eyes of the enemy. Or even the mask and the anti-chemical suit, this airtight uniform that must never leak.

With the opening of hostilities on the land front, the strategic detachment is out of place: now it is finally necessary to act, to advance to tactical contact with the other, search him out, flush him out and kill him. And from this the horror of a meeting where it is not only the case that *the other is my death* but also where the milieu, the environment, is hostile, on the ground with its traps and its mines, or in the air with its climate, since it is now the case that even the air we breathe has become the enemy. Where does this hideous suit come from, like a 'sleeping bag', not so far from those sacks sent back behind the lines during the night of lethal confrontations containing the remains of the victims. Not only have the beautiful sparkling uniforms of wars past disappeared for ever, to be replaced by the khaki work clothes of the soldiers; but now the dappled combat uniform has also disappeared into a wrapping not so different from a garbage bag, from where the soldier will see his adversary, through a window, a sort of windscreen most often misted over by his panting respiration . . .

We have all seen, on television, these *mardi gras* uniforms worn by those involved in training to avoid death from

71

asphyxiation, and this in the very moment when we are presented, in Paris, with the spring and summer fashion, on mannequins with increasingly bare bodies, made transparent by the clothing of net and gauze . . . It even seems as if our great designers have gone to the Gulf to present their new designs.

To be absent, to be not there for anybody, is what is wished for, instinctively, by those who occupy *a place apart* where danger and death lie. Whether or not they are able or wish to do it, the inhabitants of these uninhabitable places must rapidly pick out their dress, a nice little 'outfit' [*tenue de sortie*] for going out [*s'en sortir*] or for dying. A few days ago, during a broadcast concerning the coalition forces, the colonel, commander of the Senegalese contingent, declared, 'We are killing ourselves, but we do not dishonour ourselves.' What applies to the Senegalese soldiers engaged in this battle confined to the Near East will apply as well to other opposed combatants, on both sides in the next line of fire. It is not because 'those who live by the sword die by the sword' that it is necessary to debase them as we have known so well how to do for nearly forty years now.

We who are about to observe their reciprocal extermination through the telescope, through the TV telescope, let us not thus reverse the roles: we are not innocent laboratory assistants studying, analysing the viruses scientifically, microbes placed under the lens of a microscope. If the voluntary soldiers choose the mask and the costume of a hideous carnival, let us not choose, on our part, the blindfold of a self-appeased conscience. We do not share the innocence, only the guilt. If the habit makes the monk, the uniform of combat no longer makes the 'soldier' and it was ages ago that 'civilians' were fully responsible for the great military-industrial war of extermination: chemical research- ers and nuclear physicists, workers in weapons factories building Scud or Exocet missiles, laboratory workers produ- cing viruses and infectious agents of all sorts, or even those who build bunkers or gas chambers . . .

Now it is our turn, during the days that follow, to choose a mask, a costume, to assist — live, or in slightly deferred time — the death of others. Lest we blind ourselves in indif- ference or with a dubious presumption of innocence, let us choose a modest, discreet outfit, to salute those who are going to die for the UN and Saddam Hussein. It is even possible, after all, that the Gulf War will bring people and nations closer together in the future than did the nuclear peace or the deterrence that preceded it. The brothers in arms of the opposed camps are often closer to one another than to the 'officials' who have committed them to their mutual destruction.

10 February 1991

OF UNKNOWN SOLDIERS

A piece of military hardware abandoned in the snow and mud, old missiles pointed towards nowhere along a battered road, planes never used parked next to a hangar in ruins; but also forgotten aviators, living in camps worthy of a gulag, soldiers living amid military anarchy, in the rhythm of violence, of murders, theft, rape, desertion and suicide.

73

And then, what the broadcast of Jean-Claude Guidicelli about the Red Army, on Saturday 2 February, did not show: the state of maintenance and surveillance of the scientific and space material, or even that of the Russian nuclear sites.

What becomes of an army when it is no longer an army? Obviously, that army which was, not long ago, the most feared in the world has been struck by an unprecedented sort of defeat, vanquished not by an external enemy, but by its own weapons: the useless technological excess of a nuclear deterrence that dedicated its soldiers to idleness and unemployment.

Just a little more than ten years ago, it was already too late for the Red Army, when, on the brink of the disastrous invasion of Afghanistan, Marshal Gretchko, Brezhnev's Minister of Defence, declared: 'The continuing development of our armed forces is a necessity for the structure of social-ism and communism.' The proclamation to the world of the end of the 'dictatorship of the proletariat' was a done deal, Marxism had become the expiatory victim of the technolo-gies of the day, and the Russian people lost, along with their ideology, *the actual force of armies, which is a spiritual force.* Since then, the invincible warrior has been nothing more than an armoured cadaver who remains standing only by virtue of the mass of military equipment within which he has already been struck dead.[12]

How can we refrain any longer from contemplating this historical failure when we look at the televised images of the Gulf War that the Pentagon parsimoniously releases every day? It is true that the American high command is more confident since nothing up till now has refuted the

74

old Anglo-Saxon military doctrine of an army willing to risk getting caught up in a bloody land battle (particularly since it generally leaves this to its allies) and that has preferred for centuries *the war of machines over hand-to-hand combat*.[13]

Nevertheless, here too, nuclear deterrence has done its work, just as much in the army as in American public opinion, since this overarmed people find themselves disarmed before the necessity of making use of its arms, at a loss when faced with the fact that one can actually die in war and also kill an enemy with one's own hands. Such was evident from the first hours of the conflict, when several career soldiers preferred to desert with the assistance of religious organizations.

The American media have therefore been charged with preparing the public for the worst, as if taking precautions in the case of a serious illness. We will speak first of benign operations, we will effect as little damage as possible, we will go so fast that we will not feel anything, and the laser will be used to selectively hit the dangerous parties. We will also show just how precious is the life of the combatants: at the same time, an American civil Boeing airplane that crashes with some hundred passengers on board will only get a few seconds of airtime, while the accidental death of two or three GIs will be treated at length. We are thus progressively approaching the acceptance of ineluctable death; we admit that the illness is perhaps more concealed, more profound, than the first examination led us to assume. We adopt, finally, a different language; we cite now those old warriors who never die,

75

like general Patton: 'Victory is not to die for your country but that your enemy is made to die for his' (10 February 1991, on CBS).

Traditionally, a Bible is offered to each American soldier leaving for the front. Is this merely a talisman for them, or do they actually bother to open it? And if they did, I seriously doubt that it would be very good for their military valour to discover the irony of the destiny of armies and the founders of empires engaged since the beginning of time in wars of annihilation, 'only to establish vast kingdoms on the suffering of their victims in order finally to provide their booty to other conquerors, paying thus the ransom of their imperialism, in falling from global power to powerlessness, in the span of a single human life'.[14]

Readily invoking the spirit of Nebuchadnezzar, Saddam Hussein is himself, without doubt, one of these 'founders of empires' who rise up again ceaselessly from the depths of history to the detriment of humanity.

We do not know much of these soldiers, apart from the destruction they have already caused and certain gymnastics exercises performed for the official cameras. Apparently, they do not live in 1991, but in a far more remote time of war. Although possessing technology and weapons, they remain, for their commanding officers, a primary material, an instrument that exists to be employed and whose attrition is in the grander order of things, as we saw in the course of the Iran–Iraq conflict. In no way victims of deterrence, for the spiritual force is no more lacking in them than hatred, these soldiers of another age thus die like those before them, for the realization of a work that they disregard. We need not ask any more of them; television will do the rest.

11 February 1991

THE WALL OF ATLANTIS

It is no longer the Siegfried Line or the Atlantic Wall, it is the wall in the sky. Deeply buried, with only simple arches of concrete left visible above the surface of the ground, Saddam Hussein's bunkers are curiously similar to those 'stealth airplanes' that are undetectable by radar until it is too late.

A war of decoys, of ruses and camouflage of all sorts, the Gulf Conflict does not fail to unveil its charms, the discreet spells of the strategy of secrecy.

After the offensive arms — Scud, Tomahawk and B52s — here now is the hour of defensive means, the blockhouse, these subterranean shelters, that coalition soldiers on the ground are going to have to conquer one after the next, these 'grunts' [*rampants*] crawling around miserably in holes or in the sand of the battlefield, while the forces flying overhead reign supreme in the air.

We observe elsewhere in the Iraqi defensive system, casually presented recently in magazines or on television, a strange upending on the horizon: if, yesterday, we erected towers, walls or casemates for artillery, it seems today we choose to *reinforce the ground*, to strengthen its porous surface and bury fortifications as deeply as possible, as if the surface of the earth had become the last littoral, *a vertical*

77

littoral to protect against all aggression from the sky, from this atmosphere henceforth more threatening than the hydrosphere and where 'flying fortresses' reign, just as battleships and submarines dominate the sea. This includes even airfields paradoxically buried in the depths of the desert sand, like sarcophagi containing the mummies of flying machines, the Mirage F1 or Sukhoi 21.

Within these shelters, most often constructed by Europeans – Belgians, Germans or Italians (we must really wonder what Iraq would have been able to do without the support of the Soviets or Western powers) – are thus to be found the great reserve of Iraqi forces. Sheltered from the view of satellites and other means of coalition reconnaissance, Saddam Hussein's army will await resolutely the coalition's land offensive.

It is a mystery, an enigma of a hidden treasure in the desert, a sort of modern Atlantis that must be discovered quickly and at all costs to protect the coalition soldiers. Since time immemorial, the exhibition of citadels served as a deterrence – from the Great Wall of China to the Maginot Line, passing through the Roman limes,[15] fortifications supported the politics of power: it is said that they kept potential invaders of threatened nations at bay. Curiously, for some years now, the inverse has been the case: one displays one's destructive weapons and carefully dissimulates one's defensive infrastructures, while the deterrence of the potential enemy now lies solely in weapons of mass destruction, both 'conventional' and especially 'non-conventional'. There would be much to analyse concerning the future evolution of these regional conflicts, in particular, when we say to ourselves that these shelters of Saddam Hussein are anti-atomic, designed to protect hundreds of soldiers in a hostile environment, thanks to a sophisticated air filtration system.

Thus, although this 'localized' war is not even a month old, we hear the leaders, both the Americans and others, admitting that they are in favour of the utilization of a tactical atomic weapon on the front. In a recent poll taken in the USA, it has even been claimed that 44 per cent of the population would be in favour of the use of weapons of this sort if they could shorten the Gulf War and save human lives.

'Holy war or pure war?' This question that I posed on 23 August seems unfortunately to have become a reality, to the point that François Mitterrand exposed himself to open criticism by the opposition for having renounced this type of weapon.

Unbelievable! For forty years we continually repeated (this proving the point) that the use of such weapons would literally be apocalyptic, as much for the environment as for people; and suddenly, hard as it is to believe, we are acting as if such an abuse of this terror would be possible, indeed even probable.

If this tragic hypothesis were to be fulfilled in the following days, the Gulf War would be transformed, becoming soon not only a land war but, worse, a *non-conventional* war, for which it seems we are being prepared, day by day.

If this were the case, the political dimension of this regional conflict would instantly disappear, and we, powerless or nearly so, would be witnesses to the preconditions for the Third World War.

11 February 1991

OPEN WAR

Are the horrors of war merely mistakes? We might be led to believe as much from listening to commentators and certain televised journals. If this were the case, we could hardly imagine a Goya painting with these sorts of flaws.

It will prove to have taken only two laser-guided bombs hitting a bunker in the west of Baghdad, last week, to short-circuit the system of spoken precautions now in place for a month: a system of defence and representation of information that a number of journalists have established on the basis of a censorship that conceals from us the devastation, the victims of the conflict.

How is it possible today not to realize that a war is, first of all, a crescendo, *an ascent to extremes*, destined to set those who wage it on the ground against those who watch it at home? Having lived through forty years of deterrence, we have, it would seem, forgotten the atrocity of an actual war, the abomination of the desolation of dead children. Having grown accustomed to the low-grade violence of crime, or the fiction of hyperviolent films, we have forgotten the very excess of the great war of extermination that has already been seen twice in Europe in the course of the twentieth century.

Let us recall certain obvious facts: once war has been declared, there are hardly any true 'enemies' any longer, and therefore hardly any true soldiers, civil or military, actors or spectators. In other words, we will have to wait for *open war*, for the death of our own, in order to find ourselves brutally engaged in the horror and hatred of the

adversary. And from this arises the necessity for comman-
ders of the opposing camps to take account of the mounting
public disapproval from both sides of the front. Such has
been the case, over the past six months, with the Gulf War.

Patiently, cautiously, most often through interposed journalists, in Iraq and elsewhere, we have been preparing our
senses for the murderous intoxication: by little strokes at
first − the hostages − then more clearly − the nocturnal
vision of the bombardments − and, finally, dramatically −
the civilian victims of the bunker in Baghdad. Henceforth,
the way is clear, the boulevard of crime offers aversion
towards the other to all those who will soon choose hate. It
is the first lesson of every major conflict. The sole novelty:
today this lesson is administered live by television and no
longer pre-recorded in the press or on the radio.

I do not know if an image is worth more than a thousand
words, but I do know from experience that a certain image of
war is worth a soldier's enlisting for battle on the front.
Thus, war is a sort of *infantilization of societies*, which give
themselves up body and soul. A phenomenon of mimetic
training, a reciprocal apprenticeship of the horror of the
other, war is always a school, a university of shared terror
where, bit by bit, we become like our enemy by dint of
opposing them. From this comes the frightful equation of the
present situation: if Saddam Hussein has no scruples and is
preparing to use every sort of military means, including non-
conventional means, then tomorrow his UN adversaries will
become like him, and this from the moment the war has
enlarged its terrestrial horizon, in Kuwait or in Iraq. Such an
uncertain situation must cause us concern: if we so often

come to resemble those whom we fight with fury; if, as Malraux claimed, just wars never beget innocent armies; what response, what riposte shall we adopt if the Iraqi leader chooses chemical or bacteriological war, as he has promised? *Matching him to what point* — to the point of using gas, or neurotoxins? How can we hope to win the just war if the other succeeds in engaging us in injustice, a great international crime before the eyes of all? On 5 August 1972, in a letter addressed to the Minister of Culture, Jacques Duhamel, the film director Abel Gance wrote: 'Cinema was not capable of discovering its atomic bomb.' Today, by contrast, it seems indeed that television has just invented its own. With instantaneous coverage of the Gulf War, we all find ourselves in effect engaged, willingly or not, in the atrocity of the attacks; and, more importantly, we all find that we have become involved in the nature of the combat, be it 'conventional' or 'non-conventional', with the ethical risks and thus the political risks that this implies.

Let me conclude with an image, that of the double explosion of that air-fuel compression bomb that destroys not only buildings, and living bodies, but also the air, the atmosphere that we breathe . . . It would be a great shame if this weapon were to become the obligatory metaphor of this conflict, as it would suggest that the conflict was not satisfied simply with eliminating the threat of a dictator, but that it left the post-war atmosphere unlivable. Let us remember that, up to now, the great victory of the coalition was won by the non-aligned, the Israelis who refused to respond to the terrorist attacks of the Iraqi Scuds.

16 February 1991

BEHIND THE SET, BEFORE THE STRIKE

Long ago Adolf Hitler wrote, 'The idea of protection haunts and fulfils life.' If we observe the development, this winter, of the events of daily life, this is evident. Once, wars were synonymous with voyages, invasions or exiles; today, it is the inverse that has come to be the case.

Everyone to the shelters! appears to be the rallying cry, not only in the Near East, but even here in Europe. So from the beginning of the Gulf Crisis last summer, various shipping companies continue to express their frustration, having been faced with a sudden restriction of movement, particularly in the case of air shipping. At the same time, and inversely, we are witnessing the veritable launching of cable, the requests for subscriptions having doubled recently, thanks to CNN. Meanwhile, following the orders of the international business leaders, business people now avoid travel, fostering thereby the rise of audio and video-conferencing. With this anticipated retreat, we are thus witnessing the preconditions of a new type of *cocooning*, which is not heading, however, in the direction of reviving reading, since we have just about done away with book fairs, and since our publishers also complain of the collapse of sales.

Are we dealing with an incidental phenomenon, lacking real consequences, linked to the uncertainty of the future? Or is it not rather a clinical symptom, not only of economic recession but equally of a mutation of social customs, of our way of life? In order to complete this picture, we need only consider automobile manufacturing overrun by the problems of massive restructurings: 15,000 job losses in two years at

83

General Motors, comprising 15 per cent of the wage-earners of the American company, not to mention the collapse of 30 per cent of the European orders, a collapse that affects as well Mercedes, Renault and Citroën. Only the antique car shows regain their glamour, the splendour of a museum that does not bode well for the future of domestic automobility. As proof, consider this Saturday evening past, 16 February, and the monstrous highway traffic jam in the region of Lyon, where tens of thousands of holiday-makers were stuck on the autoroute with no way out.

Even if the Gulf Conflict and the effect of a live tele-presence have played a role in accelerating events in this current return to domesticity [*retour au foyer*], at the end of the 1980s the retreat had already taken shape with the unprecedented development of information technology and real-time telecommunications. The electronic control of the battlefield there, the automated control of the home environment here: these two movements are mutually reinforcing, as the electronic technologies in the home are the direct inheritance of the rise of the tele-technologies of war (that is, of military intelligence).

How is it possible not to recognize the promotional character of this Gulf Conflict; not only in the domain of weapons but also in that of the 'telematic' equipment of our household appliances, in our accommodations? If information is at this point scandalously controlled by the belligerents of the two camps, it is indeed because it will be the most important aspect of the 'post-industrial' future of the world.

Finally, one of the results of this confused conflict of influence is the promotion of the *real time of exchanges*, such as that seen in the *program-trading* of Wall Street and London that was at the vanguard of this powerful phenomenon until the stock market crash in 1987: to control oil reserves, the energy supply certainly of tomorrow's mobility, but also the temptation to control the absence of mobility, *the effect of the standstill* associated with the control of the home environment that is beginning somewhat to take shape everywhere, as much in Japan as in the USA.

At the precise moment when we are recommending to the people of the Near East to fit out an airtight den, a room carefully battened down as shelter from chemical weapons, and to keep their radios and televisions on at all times, we are also developing *tele-shopping* and *tele-work* from home, a den of retreat from usual human activities, where *tele-action* completes *tele-audition* or common television.

So, we arrive at the electronic suit, the famous 'data costume' of virtual space (cyberspace) that is itself a recreational offshoot of research into the future combat outfit, the supple spacesuit that will allow soldiers of the year 2000 not only to protect themselves against gas or radiation but also to be here and elsewhere *at the same time* (in other words, in real time), by virtue of a system of remote telecommunications that will allow them to eliminate their invisible adversary without moving physically, thanks to sensors and other instantaneous tele-detectors.

A vision of the future for a tele-existence 'in common', where everyone will be obliged to be absent in order to be present, no longer to move, to stand still for the *live* camera in order to advance without advancing, and finally, to arrive without going anywhere.

'Finish, oh! Finish everything', wrote Samuel Beckett, our dear prophet of misfortune, who died in the moment of the collapse of the Berlin Wall.

18 February 1991

THE PLACE OF DEATH

A fixed image is worth more than a thousand words, but an animated image of war is worth a soldier enlisting for battle on the front. This is apparently what the French military leadership believes and also SIRPA,[16] who decided to prohibit the battlefield of the Gulf to our civilian cameras and to allow access to only one photographer and one representative of the written press, leading, on 17 February, to the boycott by television journalists.

This does not just date from yesterday, for it was long ago that General Westmoreland brought a suit against the American network CBS for its 'bad conduct' during the Vietnam War and its 'news gone mad'; and also long ago that the joint director of the British public network replied to Margaret Thatcher, during the war in the Falkland Islands, in a release that stated: 'BBC reports the news, not propaganda . . .'

But what is news and what is propaganda? Who knows anymore, when faced with this new 'image capacity' of *live TV*, which, following Gorbachev and his advisers, Saddam Hussein used and abused even more than he did his infantry and artillery, right from the first days of the Gulf Crisis.

86

'To take photographs is to disobey,' said Robert Dois-
neau. The great change with *live broadcasts* is that the journalist on board the 'info-vehicle' no longer has the choice,
no longer holds the wheel, *he is seated in the place of death*
and his position is henceforth the same as that of the tele-
spectator, since he sees the images at the same time, in the
very moment when both sides are in the balance. Seduced
by the intoxication of speed, journalists first understood this
instantaneity as a liberation of the news. As one of them
said (it would seem a century ago!), 'The faster the news
goes, the more it is viewed. This works well when current
developments take off, as in Romania or Berlin . . .'

Finally, the retro broadcast on Channel 3, *Histoire paral-
lèle*,[17] proves the most enlightening in connection with this
news crisis that, for the moment, is confused with that of the
Gulf. When we watch those old newsreels of the Second
World War, we have less the impression of watching a news
journal than a good old film, frequently with very precise
editing, a musical track and a lyrical commentary, not to
mention the occasional 'extra' with lots of talent . . . It
would seem that those soporific films of the Pentagon and
CNN were, somehow, victims of Jean-Luc Godard and those
who confused cinema with video-surveillance.

During the First World War, the battlefield was already
prohibited to film-makers and civilian photographers, who
were subject to suspicion of espionage (they made an exception for D. W. Griffith!). But in the 'armed peace' that
followed this fatal conflict, a new phenomenon arose, and
everything was designed, on the contrary, to make contact
with and mobilize millions of movie-goers, who would soon

87

be the fodder for a war effort without precedent. There was thus no longer a divergence between propaganda and news, since, in the cinema, *everything was nothing more than propaganda*. From the cinema trains[18] of the Russian Revolution to the New Deal of Roosevelt's economic war or the English documentary movement, there were no assistants assigned to prevent the fusion-confusion of the civilian and military cameras: Dziga Vertov, Cavalcanti, David Lean, Leslie Howard or John Ford, who, on the brink of the Pacific war, filmed, on board cargo boats, the defences and the access points to the great Asian ports, under the cover of researching locations for future filming! He would be named, not long after, to head the OSS (Office of Strategic Service).

Roberto Rossellini dedicated himself to fascist propaganda before diving into neo-realism with the liberation. Joseph Goebbels, director of Nazi propaganda and cinema, had been not only a journalist but also a scriptwriter. As for the Pentagon, it was at once a producer and distributor of 'semi-documentary' films that were an amalgam of authentic documents and fictive scenes produced by Frank Capra, Joris Ivens, Robert Flaherty, Fred Zinnemann, etc.

This sort of 'united front' lasted in the USA until 1948, the year of the declaration of the Cold War by President Truman, but also of the *true rise of independent television*. McCarthyism attempted in vain to suffocate this vague independence and, shortly after came the first military and media defeat of the Americans in Vietnam.

To have the first word as opposed to the last, such is the rule of the televisual war declared by Mikhaïl Gorbachev two years ago, a new electronic blitzkreig war [*guerre éclair élec-tronique*], in which Westerners have been, up to the present, relegated to the place of death.

21 February 1991

THE ANTICIPATED RETREAT

If, as Sun Tse said, military force is ruled by its relation to the apparent, *to vanish into thin air* is not necessarily synonymous with flight or evasion, but may be seen as a sidestepping, in the sense of boxing. To leave one's front lines empty before an attack long planned in advance is a tactic as old as trench warfare. Obviously, in this war where vision machines dominate, lures and dissimulations have become decisive, as opposed to actual weapons.

Moreover, *if that which is seen is already lost*, then, inversely, everything that is dissimulated to view, to the awareness of the enemy, automatically has the advantage. The future is therefore a great black-out, from radio silence to countermeasures of all sorts, electronic and otherwise, including the centralized control of the means of mass communication (i.e., the pools of journalists), who are themselves the necessary counterpart to this business of military appearances. Thus the historical *journée des dupes*[19] of the Ancien Régime is, in this very moment, succeeded by the false day [*faux jour*] of the Gulf War. Radar coverage, electronic control of the battlefield or the *live* coverage of events by the media, all this is nothing other than the strategic organization of a gigantic making-over of facts: that is, of

89

a menacing blinding, a blinding of which everyone, civilian or military, is the potential victim, and moreover most often a consenting victim.

But returning to the course of recent events, let us go back in order to avoid the myopia of real time: last week, following the pollution of the sea, the Persian Gulf, came the pollution of the air, of the atmosphere over Kuwait. Launched with Star Wars weapons systems, it is no longer enough that this conflict *transforms night into full day*, with the use of infrared vision or diverse means of intensifying light; the inverse has also been realized on the Iraqi side: *transforming the day into blackest night*, by the masking effect of a cloud 300 kilometres long.

In addition to having extinguished the fires in the expectation of aerial bombardments, all of a sudden *the sun is extinguished*! The new black-out extinguishes the very brilliance of day, effectively barring the aerial and spatial vision of the enemy. Smoke generators are no longer considered enough to mask a movement, an anticipated retreat; instead, the meteorological system, the cloud cover of a whole country, is now to be modified by igniting a hundred oil wells.

The smoke screen was no longer a 'tactical' but rather a 'strategic' exercise affecting the fate of the UN offensive, since it could not be met with anything but a 'symbolic resistance', so to speak, forcing the leaders of the coalition to change their war plans and attack Iraq itself.

Probably effective, before or during the Soviet–Iraqi negotiations of last Thursday, with the retreat of Saddam Hussein's army, they could do nothing more than leave behind them military squads with orders for destruction and summary executions of Kuwaitis.

A dark Sunday, in every sense of the term: both for an invincible armada spilling out into a desert bereft of the principal forces of an enemy who abandoned on the ground some barbed defences to create an illusion here or there, and for the soldiers sacrificed to the rear guard, while the Iraqi 'Republican Guard' thus retained enough force to allow it to manoeuvre, on Monday morning, in the south of Iraq.

On the evening of this subterfuge, Radio Baghdad, relayed by CNN, finally announced that the Iraqi government would accept UN resolution 660 and withdraw from Kuwait, leaving to the USSR the task of proposing a new peace plan for the Near East.

A good example of a stratagem that bodes ill for the future, unless in the end we admit, with Freud, that the future is just an illusion!

26 February 1991

HEAD HELD HIGH?

I remember the Spanish Civil War, the refugee children in the south of France with whom I went to class. It was a war-laboratory where everyone was making preparations for war, their strategies for mass extermination. A local conflict that would serve as the prelude to the world war of my childhood. In the magazines, the comics showed strange missiles flying over the towns they were to destroy. Flash Gordon was thus preparing us for the Blitzkrieg.

Today, video games have replaced the illustrations, and the pilot of the F15 succeeds Brick Bradford, but it is the same war: an experimental war that prepares public opinion for other terrors of greater magnitude. In fact, for more than a month, the habit of transforming the little screen of the video monitor has been gradually creating an addiction to these dangerous games.

Meanwhile, judging from the line that formed early in the morning in front of certain stores specializing in these war games, we can assess the impact of this conflict on the public mentality. Pacifist or militarist, each is inevitably contaminated by this 'drug for the eyes' where virtual and actual realities are confused, the problem being no longer 'how to see the world?' [*comment voir le monde?*] but first 'how to see the impure?' [*comment voir l'immonde?*].

Yesterday, a flight simulator; today, a war simulator. When will the true information of facts and the virtual information of news programmes for the 'general public', become interactive? At that point, as an amateur video-strategist told us, *a war game will reveal more about a conflict than the press.*

Faced with this situation, the Anglo-Saxon adage 'wait and see' becomes obsolete. Henceforth, it will be necessary to see without waiting, to see more quickly, no matter what, no matter when, no matter where ... including even the soldiers on the front who are carried away with this mystification, in abandoning themselves, it would seem, to the delights of the electronic game. During a recent trip, some

Japanese friends shared with me this revelation: 'We don't want the Americans to win the war, but only to have engaged us in *an experience.*'

To win or lose the conflict, for a people, is one thing; to see oneself transformed into a population guinea pig, a laboratory rat, is another. The Spanish Civil War to start the Second World War, the atomic bomb to end it: two experimental moments that contributed significantly to the increased power of extermination, on the one hand, thanks to the systematic use of air power against unarmed populations (Guernica before Rotterdam or Coventry) and, on the other hand, with the first use of nuclear weapons against Hiroshima and Nagasaki.

We know what came next: an 'arms race' for nearly a half-century, the rise of a military-industrial complex that depleted the economies of the nations involved and contributed to the overarming of certain countries such as Iraq today. The loop thus loops back from the brutality of the Gulf War to the experimentation of the Spanish Civil War. A major conflict, less by dint of its geopolitical dimensions than by its technologies and logistics, the Iraqi–UN war has already all the characteristics of a preface, of a theatrical overture for an *ecological war*, long hypothetically strategized, in order to extend the very notion of 'total war'.

Consequently, behind the escalation of this electronic war in the Near East is silhouetted the spectre of a conflict the repercussions of which would involve more a question of creating a hostile environment for the enemy than controlling the territory devastated by combat, and this, we note, in both the opposed camps in this already sterile region of the earth.

Thus, in the wake of the various oil slicks, the systematic pollution of the Persian Gulf, we learn that nearly 500 oil-producing wells are the victims of the flames, and that this atmospheric pollution extends now for over 40,000 square kilometres.

A vision of the future: when this conflict is forgotten, we will still have news from the front. In order to assess the condition of these places, we will no longer watch CNN-live, but rather meteorological updates. Day after day, month after month, the Meteosat satellite will show us, above Kuwait, or Iraq or Saudi Arabia, *the dirty war in real time*, a truly grand prefiguration of the 'nuclear winter' forecast by the analysts of so-called collateral damage.

27 February 1991

A WAR OF RUSES

Great warriors never die, they simply fade away. It is probably the same with great wars: they never end, but haunt our memory and leave victims among our recollections. What, then, are we going to forget of this war that was more intensive than extensive? A grave question of consequences for the future, the long-term effects of a conflict that was, from the first, a conflict of interpretation between two cultures, two histories. In this region of the world, where the Tower of Babel once stood, we are effecting the greatest of confusions, the greatest possible disguising of facts.

In addition to the systematic polluting of the sea and air in the warring countries, there is the unprecedented polluting of the media that will leave its trace on our dispositions, our mentality, on the audience that is indispensable to an independent media. Finally, the first victims of this Gulf War will have been the journalists and those who listen to or watch them broadcast live. Henceforth, their credibility fades away, weakened, and the confusion occasioned by this shoddy treatment of the news will return ineluctably in the ill will, the loss of the audience, as we see already in the USA, where certain CNN reporters were perceived as traitors in the employ of Iraq, just as in the Maghreb the same reporters appeared, inversely, as the 'lackeys of American imperialism'.

As in repetition syndrome of the victims of terror, which causes them constantly to relive the horror of bombings, tele-spectators will be distinctly prone to prolonging their disapproval vis-à-vis the handling of news by discredited reporters, and this, we will remember, has already been the case for a year now, or more precisely since the business with the Romanian revolution.

Prepared by a total control of the electromagnetic environment above Iraq, and by a complete jamming of telecommunications that must have made Radio Baghdad inaudible, it was necessary that the Gulf War begin, on the night of 16 January, with the destruction of the army's communications centre, situated in the Iraqi capital, the laser-guided bomb launched towards its objective in total impunity by a 'stealth' airplane.

In this conflict where, for the first time in history, the various satellites played a major role, the control of communications outweighing the control of the geographical territory of the enemy, the five weeks of aerial bombardment demonstrated less the will to raze towns (as was once the case) than the will to eliminate the entire Iraqi communication and telecommunication infrastructure – the ground offensive itself becoming a simple formality, a sort of postscript to a 'total electronic war' that was bound to influence all of public opinion, thanks to the control of the various media by the Pentagon.[20]

Rather like the great centre of coalition command, dubbed C^3I – a true control of military operations situated in the USA – the strategic leaders of this conflict will prove to have continuously monopolized the real information and focused to their advantage the most important news from the front, to the disadvantage not only of the enemy, as is fair in war, but also, and perhaps especially, to that of the coalition reporters working in the pools.

I would wager that this lesson will not be forgotten and that this monopolizing of information begun by CNN will be repeated, this time in times of peace: consider, on this subject, the crisis of the old international press agencies. Meanwhile, since 1989, a year of great geopolitical and strategic upheaval, the uncertainty concerning the future is such – in the Soviet Union, in Europe and in the entire Mediterranean basin – that certain leaders might well wish to justify this sort of control, this sort of media censorship, by virtue of the necessity of avoiding a panic of public opinion and the disastrous consequences of a lapse in security that would ensue from the economy of international trade and even from simple tourism.

Whatever else it may be, we will not soon forget the military parade of colonels, generals and admirals, coming day after day to comment sententiously upon the events on television, and this in the very moment when we must deplore, once again, 'the silence of intellectuals', as if, henceforth, the *Grand Muette*[21] were no longer the army, but rather the intelligentsia!

Since it is indeed necessary (is it not?) to fill this 'silence', why not make a call to professionals rather than amateurs?

To conclude, even while the highly technological army of tomorrow will need skilled soldiers rather than conscripts, I would wager that on television there will soon be a need for volunteers to ensure that there will be live coverage of military or police events!

5 March 1991

THE GREAT BLACK-OUT

'Is not the world just a magic lantern?' wondered Schopenhauer, nearly two centuries ago. Due to the Gulf Crisis, a conjuring trick executed before our eyes, for several months we have not seen a great deal of this world there on our television screens. Obscured, on the one side, is the Saudi desert, with the great black-out ordered by the Pentagon; on the other side is Saddam Hussein and his army that has become invisible. But also obscured is all of what, from near or far, could undermine the morale of the people concerning the conflict: recession, unemployment, urban riots, the balkanization of Eastern Europe and the almost complete disappearance of political debates. Another unforeseen eclipse was that of the planet Mars, as the photographs, taken at the time by the NASA space probe, were not broadcast.

Sure, we were concerned, but the television reporters were no longer there to make it worse, to increase our day-to-day anxieties; we were on a vacation from images, to the degree that many tele-spectators, who at the beginning of the conflict were glued to their sets, were now wearied and preferred to turn them off.

If, in Europe, we did not miss the missing images, the Americans, after the hostage affair, came to the conclusion that there had been too many and wished, by a great majority, that the government would again reinforce the censorship. They were convinced that their television had become perfidious, that it had been infiltrated by the enemy and was serving as a transmission channel for Saddam Hussein. A portion of the population thus decided voluntarily to refuse images, news and commentaries, for the sake of 'patriotism', in order not to become the consenting victim of enemy propaganda diffused through its own media, with the assistance of journalists accused of colluding with the enemy. On the front, the American army had meanwhile taken the lead in stopping and provisionally interning several reporters and press photographers vaguely likened to spies.

We must wonder today whether, in the long run, if this attitude of collective rejection persists, it does not risk turning into a new sort of protectionism, a negation pure and simple of the need to be informed that will lead, sooner

or later, to the extinction of public opinion, and consequently to the end of a certain form of democracy. It is
frightening, as is the case currently, to confuse the message
and the messenger, to confuse the actions of journalists
(every day more and more threatened) and those of the *live
technologies* that have been used and abused for several years
now, especially since the inflight explosion of the American
space shuttle *Challenger*, on 28 January 1986, a catastrophe
broadcast live by CNN, a media performance that established the global power of the Atlanta network.

In many Western countries, it seems that household appliances claim more victims than the automobile. We are
never suspicious enough of technical objects, of all this
domestic fauna, these strange aids that we introduce into
our private homes with a certain lack of awareness and
among which the television, too, can cause some major accidents. After the Watergate scandal that cost President
Richard Nixon his office, we no longer pay much attention
to the number of nasty tricks that instruments of communication have played on those who believe they have mastered
them. If we return to CNN, it is publicly known that Ted
Turner's network is the favourite of such important figures
as Bush or Gorbachev, or even Fidel Castro; but it is generally forgotten that it is the man himself in Atlanta who
presented the services of his network to these heads of
state. Yet there are poisoned gifts, and times when, as
Virgil said regarding the Trojan horse, one must beware the
Greeks and their presents; and we may, for example,

99

wonder whether, ultimately, during the Gulf Crisis, Saddam Hussein did not turn out to be the pawn of his favourite network . . .

Just the same, the American public should certainly be more wary of the *behaviourism inherent in the technologies of instantaneous broadcasting* than of the unfortunate journalists of CBS or CNN disoriented in the Saudi desert. Indeed, why do we say 'hello'[22] when we pick up the phone; won't the greetings that follow be sufficient? The word passes automatically across our lips, as if the phone forces us to say it. With regard to the telephone, the painter Degas remarked, 'It rings to you and you come.' Why not, when answering, say: 'What may I say is calling?' like the comic at the beginning of the twentieth century.

Being from the upper middle class, Edgar Degas understood that the *signal* of the long-distance transmission was an order – a feature of domestic life, since the bell was at that time used not only to open doors but also to direct from a distance the movements of workers and servants in vast estates, servants trained to adopt the bearing desired by the master of the estate, who alone was fit to give orders. Forced to remain silent by this unilateral system of entering into communication, these servants in general possessed only a reduced vocabulary of about fifty words.

When in 1974 President Nixon wished to create a system to directly turn on the television sets of all American citizens from the chair of the executive, in order, he said, to enable notification at home, he was only reproducing the peremptory process of domestication, but this time on the level of an entire continent. The project was rejected by a

Congress that found this 'democracy', abruptly reduced to the administration of an electronic stimulus, frightening, as they recognized that in such a state they would no longer be needed.

Indeed, Richard Nixon was perhaps trying simply to present himself as up to date with the technological capabilities of the USA, notably after the success of the transmission from the Apollo 11 flight, broadcasting live, to more than five hundred million tele-spectators in the world, the first steps of an American man on the moon, in July 1969 ... Was the project of *home alert* not essentially realized through 'the authorization for development' granted in 1972 by the Federal Communications Commission to cable television?

With CATV,[23] the great depopulation of the mass media had begun. Following the example of broadcast television, cable television no longer wished to be considered as mere entertainment, but rather as a domestic service, a 'means of communal broadcasting' approaching a public service. Cable television no longer acted on its own, but became a *passive technology*, programmable like any other household appliance. Tele-entertainment and its actors would be progressively replaced by tele-shopping, tele-action and interactive games, giving rise to CATV's initial refusal to pay royalties to any party, a refusal that spoke volumes concerning the actual contents of such projects.

In a fashion not unlike the fate of mass cinema in the 1940s, television such as we know it was bound to disappear: it no longer entertains us, it is less and less the vehicle of culture or marketing politics, and it will soon cease to

101

be a convenient means of information. Beyond the Atlantic, there are already new systems of tele-command that allow the tele-spectator not only to change the channel at will (as is the case now), but also to manipulate the document as it airs, thanks to a control by which automatic cameras spread about at different angles can be remotely adjusted. A football match or an automobile race will thus be viewed live from five or six different angles, chosen one after the other by the tele-spectator himself. With such a system, not only the sportscaster and the cameraman, but even the director, in a way, have disappeared, *transported into the home*.

The progress of interdependence that already characterized CATV, made still worse by the use, around 1980, of the personal computer, was inevitably bound to change the representation of the Gulf Crisis. The cinema-war of the 1940s, and the Vietnam War televised in deferred time or the non-declared war of the nuclear status quo (the atomic game that, according to H. Kahn, was destined to play out on forty-four squares), were all succeeded in the end by the *disappearance* of a miniaturized world war, fought and won in a few hours.

To the surprise of tele-spectators, the most important thing about the Gulf Conflict would necessarily remain invisible, despite the incredible means of communication in place. For the television networks with their 'star reporters' were obviously falling behind the war: live news and its dangerous capacity to change public opinion instantly by presenting material that was more or less authentic no longer corresponded with the passivity of the new media. Burned by Gorbachev's and Saddam's exploits in this domain, the Pentagon decided to neutralize the acceleration of the technologies of communication and to install and screen a system that was better matched to the new psychology of American tele-spectators (for, let us not forget, the UN partners of the USA were treated by the Pentagon with significant contempt during the conflict).

If we accept that this was only a *prelude to the establishment of a new world order*, indeed to future Star Wars, why not suppose that, every moral objection aside, the activity of the military-industrial and scientific machine could replace, on screen, military deeds, *since on the battlefield itself it is already done, and since, henceforth, technology will be in command of strategy*.

Freed from news agencies and other boring commentators, war could be conducted in total abstraction; it would be shown in people's homes, not in the manner of some sort of Nintendo game, but rather, here once more, as a sort of production, presented again in a way in which there could be no definite calculation of the odds; a free-market enterprise capable of making a profit from major accidents and ecological risks, rather like Lloyd's of London, the old gambling den and betting society, that became, over the course of centuries, an international society of classification and identification, based on the tracking of navies and their shipwrecks, across the world's oceans . . .

Poorly adapted to the spirit of the times, the image of acts of courage would give way to a *pathology of the game*

103

linked to the evaluation of the cost of arms and the material losses, as well as to the benefits that would ensue, as today, in Kuwait.

The photographs of the mutilated bodies of the dead and wounded would be suppressed not only to avoid a humanitarian uprising like that during the Vietnam War, but also because in a game, in principle, one does not die; in the case of Saddam, we make him out to be a cheat, one who, unlike Bush, does not respect the rules of the game of war as decreed by international conventions, and who resorts to illegal weapons that do not kill in the same fashion as the others. It is from this that the secret strategy adopted by the Pentagon derives all its meaning, since the mechanism of every game of chance, including that of war, is distributed in time between the extreme poles of the seen and the unseen, or rather, of the not yet seen.

Given that in America business means business, thanks to passive technologies, real war would function in the future, no longer at the service of the old system of 'patriotic loans' (advocated by those in cinema, such as Charlie Chaplin or Douglas Fairbanks, haranguing, in 1917, the enthralled masses of Wall Street), but rather in the manner of the famous *program trading* that is now getting out of hand: *the international exchange of weapons* where tele-spectators think themselves the *golden boys*, with all the risks of the apocalyptic economic collapse that this may suppose. Are not the gambling addicts of Vegas already becoming adapted to placing multiple bets, thanks, precisely, to the many cabled screens that incite them to follow instinctively the play of several games at once?

Thus the tele-spectator would be progressively trained to deny the very existence of a distant war, with its cortège of horrors and all-too-real destruction, just as we once chose to ignore the destructive impact of colonies and then of decolonization, as long as each gained a profit. The tele-spectator could then become the dream partner of a *Pentagon-capitalism* that emerges triumphantly from a conflict in which its primary objective would be to surpass its true European, Russian or Japanese competitors in the sale of weapons of communication, its Iraqi pseudo-enemy being relatively insignificant by comparison.

We are indeed far from the Media Eden dreamed of thirty years ago by McLuhan, or even by Ted Turner, hoping, himself, to capture the promise of American technology with the perpetual expansion of the CNN empire. These last years, the Atlantan seems to have succeeded where Richard Nixon had so dismally failed: the couple Turner–Jane Fonda could even be aiming, it is said, for the White House.

Nevertheless, despite the exclusivity that was accorded him by the Pentagon, the increase in the number of the faithful and his publicity revenues, the *live* TV of Ted Turner lost the Gulf War, because the American high command, wishing to shelter the American public from weapons of communication, had decreed that the 'real time' of the operations under way could no longer be the 'present time' of the tele-spectators seated before the little screen. This represented a subtle censorship beyond that of images, being instead that of the instantaneity of the *remote signal* and its mobilizing power; it was this that explained the disaffection of the public with what should be the 'actual' news of the moment [*une actualité*], but is not.

After the archaic *passive defence* and the lights-out of the great cities of the Near East, intended to protect the citizens from the enemy bombings, *passive television* now claims to protect the world population from the light-speed of cathode attacks: the world, during the conflict, would be perceived in slow motion; even the forecasts of meteorological satellites flying over the Gulf would be held back, and their broadcast delayed in order to withhold information from the enemy; with regard to the photographs of the planet Mars, NASA will release them much later . . . fifteen days after the cessation of hostilities.

2 April 1991

IV

June 1991: Desert Screen

DESERT SCREEN

'*Everything that happened in Iraq and Kuwait demands a re-examination of the entire anti-aircraft defence of the country,*' declared the Minister of Defence of the Soviet Union, Marshal Dimitri Iazov, just after the cease-fire, thus confirming the words, ten years earlier, of Admiral Gorchkov: '*The victor of the next war will be the one who knew best how to exploit the electromagnetic spectrum.*'

For the first time in history, even if the airplane had not put an end to war as the strategists of the past were hoping, aerial and orbital war prevailed over classical terrestrial combat, so much so that we witnessed, in the last hours of this war, some forty Iraqi soldiers surrendering to an airplane without a pilot, an aerial reconnaissance *drone* with a three-metre wingspan, equipped with a simple video camera – the future vision of this *logistic of electro-optic perception* that allowed soldiers, under shelter at their consoles, to take enemy prisoners without having to move, solely by the panic produced by the overflight of a scaled-down model!

A conflict that begins with the launching of programmed robotics, Tomahawk cruise missiles, and that ends with the surrender of enemy soldiers to a scale model of a *tele-piloted* aerial reconnaissance.[1] A good parable ... but is there not something comparable regarding public opinion, those millions of tele-spectators who are themselves finally taken in by the misleading synopses of a television controlled entirely by the army?

The war just suspended in the Near East will have been marked by such a significant number of innovations of every sort (strategic and tactical) that it must be seen henceforth as a conflict of pure experimentation, *a promotional war*, where the technological aspect prevails over the political and economic aspects, the consequences in these domains being very much open to debate.

More *intensive* than actually extensive, despite the foreseeable damage to the future equilibrium of the Middle East, the 'Persian Gulf War' will have been, in the end, a *scaled-down world war*, a sort of model or miniaturization of what could tomorrow be the total war; a conflict that *will* no longer even require the use of 'non-conventional' weapons to be economically, and, above all, ecologically disastrous.

Capable, henceforth, of *miniaturizing the world*, after having succeeded in miniaturizing its components (the paths and objects that it contains), so-called conventional war has become today, in its turn, global and planetary, thanks to the speed and to the modes of delivery of the weaponry employed by the armed forces: aerial and spatial forces operating primarily in the domain of electromagnetic waves. *The first stealth war [guerre furtive] in history*, the war of real time will have succeeded in implementing not only the stealth of its means, of its offensive weapons and the strategy of their employment on the Near Eastern battlefield, but also the total control of its public representation, on the global level.

Thus, the military environment is no longer so much a *geophysical* one of the real space of battles (terrestrial, maritime, aerial, etc.) as a *microphysical* one of the real-time electromagnetic environment of real-time engagement, in times of peace or war, as we saw during the blockade of Iraq that preceded the opening of hostilities and where the essential elements of the spatial and aerial systems were set up.

All the research of the past twenty years on 'low radar signature', the famous stealth technology [*furtivité*], will have given this conflict its meaning, historic in more than name, particularly in the domain of a military perception just now become sovereign.

As *detection* and *deception* henceforth form the foundational couplings of the American *air–land battle* strategy, the low probability of the detection of the weapons and other vectors of attack constitute an advantage of which no one wishes to be, nor can now afford to be, deprived. Thus, with the unceasingly augmented precision of *intelligent munitions*, the question of remote detection becomes crucial: *if that which is seen is already lost*, it is necessary to block at all costs long-range tele-detection, or at the very least, only to reveal one's presence as late as possible. From this revolutionary pursuit comes, militarily speaking, a *physical form* of the material of war (planes, missiles, tanks, etc.) that depends nearly exclusively on its *remote image*, its 'radar echo' or 'thermal signature'. As all characteristics of the instruments of combat are henceforth subjected to this categorical imperative of a *long-distance non-detection* (velocity, manoeuvrability, agility, etc.), the central concept of this new war game becomes 'first look, first shot, first kill'.

It is therefore no longer only a matter of implementing any sort of *ruse de guerre*, camouflage or dissimulations intended to fool the adversary as to the nature of military objects. Even if the tactics of passive decoys were used extensively by the Iraqis, these nevertheless amounted to only a minor aspect of this type of conflict, the strategic mutation being infinitely more significant, since it is now a matter of *reducing the dimensions of the envelope of detection* of the weapons systems engaged in combat in the midst of an electromagnetic environment that has become more important than the space in which the war machine, nevertheless, continues to move.

Here lies the technological revolution of this war in the Gulf: the question of the STEALTH [*FURTIVITÉ*] of the *matériel tends to supplant that of the* SPEED [*RAPIDITÉ*] of the weaponry with the greatest velocity, be it missile or combat aircraft. In fact, since seeing the enemy first and keeping him in view constitutes a decisive advantage, justifying tactics of surprise and therefore the 'first shot', the 'absolute' speed of the waves of electromagnetic detection prevails henceforth over the 'relative' speed of the supersonic or hypersonic flying object. To no longer *lose sight* of the enemy is thus to *gain* the upper hand, or indeed even to win the conflict, this war in which the disappearance from sight tends to prevail over the power of conventional or nonconventional explosives.

When intelligent munitions, tanks or planes of air supremacy are subjected to the imperatives of a delayed or

110

deferred detection, other sorts of technical difficulties arise: a conflict between the specifically aerodynamic necessities of the piloted vehicle that allow for good manoeuvrability, always necessary during close combat, and the necessities — and these are new — let's call them icodynamics[2] — of a 'low radar signature', of a low probability of detection during its approach. *The image in real time* of the supersonic aircraft prevails from a distance over the form of least aerodynamic resistance; in other words, over the real space of the design of its cockpit and airfoil.

It is almost as if the image in the mirror were suddenly modifying our face: the electronic representation on the screen, the radar console, modifies the aerodynamic silhouette of the weapon, the virtual image dominating in fact 'the thing' of which it was, until now, only the 'image'.

Therefore, the immediate and remote presentations of the flying object tend to be indissolubly confused. The radar echo induces the geometry of the weapon, of the aircraft, giving it its very form, its electromagnetic signature on a 'terminal' determining the profile, the mass and even the very nature of the absorbent coating of the war machine.

Faced with the significance of the *screen of control* that has become decisive for the stature, the scope and the very performance of the diverse vectors of land and air weapons, we may more easily infer the eminently strategic function of the *central control of information* and military intelligence; this network that henceforth reunites the collection of multiple screens, these monitors that make up the latest C^3I military command post implemented for the first time in history, during the Gulf War, by the American armed forces.

111

On a lesser level, there is something comparable in the intelligent cockpit of the last generation of combat planes that becomes the nucleus around which one designs the motor performance of the jets: their instrument panels instantaneously display sensors distributed over the super-structure of the aircraft. Designed to guarantee maximum visibility for its pilot and therefore an immediate awareness of his situation, the display of the cockpit takes on, for him alone, the capacity 'first look-first kill' now essential to the survival of the weapon. Thus, the function of 'arms' [*arme*] becomes integrally that of the 'eye'; more exactly, that of an electro-optical acquisition of targets that prevails over the range and destructive capabilities of anti-aircraft defences or other measures. From this arise the research and considerable progress in the domain of sensors and other *remote detectors* utilizing various types of electromagnetic radiation, such that today more than 99 per cent of micro-electronic production consists of ultra-sensitive sensors, a precondition of an increasingly generalized tele-action.

This profound transformation of war and its armaments, where 'communication' (detection, guidance) prevails both over 'obstruction' (armouring, decoys, etc.) and 'destruction' (explosives, munitions, etc.), has at its origin the development of a totally integrated computer architecture with very high-speed, integrated circuits, while a significant improvement in the software manages not only the cockpit but also all the avionics of the fighter plane;[3] the practical result being a new capacity to collect and integrate enormous quantities of data provided by the multiple sensors that thereby give the pilot a complete and instantaneous image of his *current and unfolding* environment.

Henceforth, on land as in the sky, the environment is no longer the 'geophysical' one traversed or flown over, but rather first the 'microphysical' environment of the control in real time of the different parameters of combat.

The strategic and political importance of the control of public and private televisions in the war of *real time*, even beyond that of the *Gulf*, is now more evident than ever.

The news pool under the sway of the Pentagon performs a key role[4] in this stealthful and intensive conflict where tele-communication satellites will have played a prominent role both during the course of operations and in the presentation of news in the mass media. Weapons are tele-guided towards their targets by laser or enhanced video, necessitating an extreme dissimulation, or else the passive decoys much utilized by the Iraqis with familiar results — tanks, planes or Scud missiles, instantaneously tele-detected by satellites and other aerial reconnaissance devices, such as the AWACS (Airborne Warning And Control System), masters of the Iraqi–Kuwaiti sky; transfiguration of the site of war and its representation, both for the opposing forces and for the tele-spectators most often duped by their usual news sources, the press and television.

The first 'absolute', if not total, war, where the control of the geophysical environment of the adversary and that of the armed forces will have given way to the control of the microphysical and electromagnetic environment of the hostile milieu. *Arms of communication* prevail for the first time in the history of combat over the traditional supremacy

113

of arms of destruction; the 'offensive' and 'defensive' themselves lose all value to the advantage of *manoeuvres of global interdiction*, or nearly so, as if this aero-terrestrial conflict will have only been the extension of nuclear deterrence by other means . . .

We will attempt therefore to identify and analyse this new 'site' [*lieu*], this so-called 'milieu', to the degree that the technologies which compose and organize it are those that tomorrow will structure the city, the *global village*.

Listen to the words of Colin Powell, Chief of the General Staff of the American Army: 'To command, it is necessary to be in control. And to be in control, it is necessary to be capable of communicating. Without intelligence, any operation is destined to failure.'

This is the reason behind the innovation in the control of the enemy environment, starting with a new electronic command post called C^3I, the true control room of the war of real time, where the responsible military principals are in continuous contact with their forces on the ground, down to the least important soldier, thanks to the orbital system of satellite transmission. The efficaciousness of aerial power, decisive in this conflict, depends upon this system of integrated command, the major role of this network being, according to General Welsch, Chief of Staff of the US Air Force, '*first with surveillance, to allow us to understand a given situation, then to bring adequate forces into play and finally to command them in a decisive manner*'.

As situational reconnaissance replaces that of any

particular objective, we enter, with the Gulf War, into a new type of conflict where the arms of interdiction and control of the battlefield will come progressively to prevail over those of mass destruction: more precisely, those of land forces.

Consequently, the more important strategic arms reduction comes to be in both the East and West, the more the air and space systems of surveillance and detection will be developed and integrated into different commands, these systems becoming prominent in the question of future politico-military supremacy.

It is therefore understandable why, from the beginning of the war, the forces of the coalition deliberately chose to asphyxiate their adversary by systematically destroying the installations of control, command and communication, the coalition air offensive being sustained throughout five long weeks, defining as its primary objective the means of telecommunication and transportation routes of the Iraqi army.

Consider again this ambiguous period entitled 'Desert Shield' (*Crise de Golfe*), a five-month period preceding the launching of the air war that lasted five weeks: essential and quite underestimated, this period would determine the fate of 'Desert Storm' (*Guerre de Golfe*), by assuring orbital control of the Iraqi territory by approximately twenty American satellites allocated to the coalition forces.

To this end, the USA will bring into play the whole of its satellite panoply, from the weaponry of optical and radar reconnaissance, to telecommunication satellites (TDRS), including their electronic listening satellites (FERRET), which intercepted, throughout these many months, all Iraqi

115

radio exchanges, the electronic intelligence (ELINT) establishing the *charting of the frequencies and wavelengths employed
by the adversary*. These operations, which began as early as
the summer of 1990 and were duly completed with U2s
carrying out high-altitude aerial reconnaissance of the Iraqi–
Kuwaiti territory, led necessarily, in January 1991, to the
systematic jamming of the communications of the Iraqi military forces.

Consequently, this vast data collection would lead, once
the UN ultimatum expired, to the jamming of the electromagnetic environment and the anti-aircraft defence systems
of Iraq. This jamming, unique of its kind by virtue of
its amplitude, affected the whole range of frequencies,
from the HF to UHF (ultra-high-frequency) and even to
Radio Baghdad, which, according to some listeners, became
inaudible.

To blind the adversarial communications and weapons
systems, the Americans employed a massive *jamming barrage*,
using ultra-powerful transmitters installed on board land and
sea vehicles, and four AWACS planes that literally saturated
the entire spectrum. A more specific jamming was secured
by 'countermeasure' devices loaded on the planes specializing in the electronic war of the 'Prowler' and 'Raven'
types. Meanwhile, the RC-135 and EC-130 planes,
manoeuvring in a circle far from the Iraqi defences, jammed
radar frequencies in order to speckle the screens with false
echoes and open the field to the F-15 fighter bombers for
the first wave of attack.[5]

Other primary objectives, pinpointed in advance by spy
satellites, included the destruction of land-to-land missile

sites, the Scud and others, as well as their centre of data transmissions. It is here that the forty Night Hawk jets, invisible to radar, entered into action, more or less simultaneously with the arrival of the Tomahawk cruise missiles at their targets. At the same time, in the Iraqi capital, the first F117A was destroying *the building that housed the communication centre of Saddam Hussein's forces*. The stealth plane was equipped with a laser that 'illuminated' the target. This inaugural operation of the air offensive was filmed by an infrared camera aboard one of the aircraft.

Having approached its target undetected, the F117A released its bomb, whose laser guidance ensured a precise impact. One of the advantages of the stealth technology is the possibility of approaching the target and directing the bomb with the greatest possible precision, an essential capacity in attacks on strongly defended targets situated deep within enemy territory, at the very heart of their forces.

Meanwhile, cruise missiles, *launched for the first time in the course of a conflict*, first from the battleships *Wisconsin* and *Missouri*, and then from the attack submarines positioned in the eastern Mediterranean, *constitute an automation of the war* whose long-range guidance system (up to 3,000 kilometres) is the most important feature, since the Tomahawk's guidance system uses a correlation of images (Digital Scene Matching Area Correlation) that represents one of the first practical applications of the future 'vision machine'. By comparing the digitized image obtained by camera of the trajectory to its objective with the scene stored in the memory of the on-board computer, the missile travels towards its target with the complementary assistance of an

117

automatic system for course-correction that takes its bearing from the Navstar network satellites. Let us recall that at a distance of about 1,300 kilometres, fifty-one out of the fifty-two missiles launched on the first night of this war hit their target, the deviation at the end of the course being only about 30 centimetres ... This degree of precision from launch to strike is made possible by a guidance and navigation system operating at extremely low altitudes (20 metres) thanks to the inertial guidance and a radar monitoring of the terrain. Even if misguided by altimetric correlation, by comparing the topography it traverses to a map in memory (programmed in advance with the information from the reconnaissance satellites), the cruise missile guides itself infallibly to the end of its course.

Note again that the communication and the precision of navigation of the *intelligent munitions* prevail over the nature of the explosive: the destructive power of the weaponry relying, in the end, on the precision of its guidance system. It is no longer necessary to carry a great quantity of explosives, and thus the paradoxical notion of the 'clean bomb', that is, in the future of the *pure weapon*.

But let us return to the reign of these satellites that one finds again everywhere in this Gulf War: both for guiding missiles or Patriot anti-missiles, the combat planes or the new attack tanks and even the 'smart bombs'. Let us first take the example of the KH (Key Hole) satellites equipped with reflecting mirrors similar to those of the Hubble space telescope[6] – except that they are aimed at the earth and not towards space. Details of less than a metre can be made out by the KH-11 and, reportedly about 30 centimetres by the

KH-12. The shots from these satellites are stored in memory, then transmitted during overflight to the *control stations*. The images are subsequently sent to the Center for Analysis of the US Air Force in Fort Belvoir, Virginia. With the KH-12, the transmission to the USA even takes place in real time, via military communication satellites.

The CIA then communicates these photographs to the White House and the NSA (National Security Agency), while the intelligence useful to the course of operations finally returns to the area of operations in Saudi Arabia, *allowing the great powers to follow, in near real time, the evolution of the situation.*

Another strategic utilization is that of Magnum-type satellites, electronic-listening satellites that would give an alert each time an Iraqi missile took off towards Tel Aviv or Dhahran. The intelligence on the Scud was then transmitted by television broadcast satellite to the Atlanta centre, for the calculation of trajectories, and then would come back, instantaneously corrected, to the launch sites of Patriot anti-missiles in Saudi Arabia or Israel, the whole process taking only a few seconds.

Recall also that the head office of Ted Turner's channel CNN is in Atlanta, which assured complete control of this conflict, or nearly, with the assent of the Pentagon; this same Pentagon that had at its disposal three enormous TDRS broadcasting systems, in geostationary orbits at an altitude of 36,000 kilometres, these systems serving to relay continuous transmissions of the other military satellites to Washington.

It is easy to see that with this conflict in 'real time', we can no longer legitimately speak of a battlefield or of a 'localized' war. Even if the land manoeuvres remain precisely situated, they are overshadowed, totally dominated by the scope of a global capacity, of an environment in which the spatio-temporal reduction is the essential characteristic. Once topical, the military conflict now suddenly becomes tele-topical: all regional wars become global precisely on account of their instantaneous control. The draconian restriction of the distances of time, between the Center for the Calculation of Trajectories situated in the USA and the different 'launch sites' of weapons in the Middle East, results in a mixing of the global and the local. The war on the ground is tied to the tactical control of the *real space* of the battle, while the terminals of strategic control are dedicated to the management of the *real time* of exchanges: for example, the decisive instant of the interception of the enemy missile with the anti-missile (witness the tele-commanded battle of the Patriots and the Scuds); or again, the different mechanized forces of land or air, equipped with satellite-controlled inertial navigation systems.

The control of general communications and of the 'microphysical' environment therefore prevails definitively over the particular 'geophysical' environment of the adversary. The attacks of the new aerial supremacy no longer focused on the destruction of cities (as was still the case in the anti-city strategy) but rather principally on the elimination of the infrastructures of communication and telecommunication, as well as certain launch sites of primary threats (missiles, tele-guided artillery, etc.).

Consequently, the true land offensive becomes a police operation, somewhat like the action of the conscripts of 'territorial armies', in contrast to the so-called 'front-line' troops. *The total electronic war* thus leads to the supremacy of this *fourth front*; the *pure* arms of communication and of instantaneous control of operations henceforth prevails over the three other fronts (land, sea and even air), and the orbital front favours, as we have just seen, the fusion of the global and the local, thanks to the prominent role of satellites. Real time, that is to say the *absolute speed* of electromagnetic exchanges, dominates real space, in other words the *relative speed* of exchanges of position, occasioned until now by offensive and defensive manoeuvres.

Hence the great metamorphosis of the 'post-modern' war: it denies both the offensive and the defensive, solely to the benefit of the control and interdiction of the battlefield, regardless of its size; the *front of instantaneous electronic intelligence* (the fourth front) becomes the equivalent of the first line of the land front during the last two 'world wars', the air front serving finally, subsequent to the considerable historical importance of naval power, to prefigure what would be the future *orbital power*.

The *third dimension* of 'atmospheric' (First World War) and 'stratospheric' (Second World War) capacities gradually loses its strategic importance in favour of an extraterrestrial or 'exospheric' capacity, which amounts to the exclusive control of the *fourth dimension*: a purely temporal dimension, that of the real time of ubiquity and instantaneity. A dimension less physical than microphysical itself typifies, or nearly so, the fourth front of the supremacy of the arms of communication.

121

Nevertheless, one element appears to be a weak point in this domain: namely, the system of interpreting enemy damages. Faced, on the one hand, with the incredible amount of data and information furnished by the diverse acquisition systems, and on the other with the massive use of decoys and underground fortifications, 'disinformation' or *deception* reached an unprecedented level. It proved extremely difficult to confirm damages caused by the aerial bombardments, and the lacunae of the BDA (Bomb Damage Assessment) were exposed, particularly the limits of its practical efficacy, from the moment that it was unable precisely to distinguish between decoys and real objectives. Moreover, the coalition air force found itself forced to deal with *potential targets*, whose exact nature was never determined because they were so well concealed in the bunkers deeply buried in the desert sands. From now on, fortification no longer consisted in putting up a barrage, in erecting some sort of wall to prevent the penetration of the enemy, but *to shield the surface*, to consider the zero level, the ground itself, as a 'front' facing the principal threats from the air and especially from space . . .

Hence the reorientation of the battlefield: no longer *towards the horizon* where the enemy will appear one day, but *towards the sky*, from which will come the threat of instantaneous detection and systematic destruction.

We can speak, therefore, in the context of this 'desert war', of the implementation on a grand scale of a genuine *strategy of deception*, not only by the allies as we have just analysed, with the massive implementation above Iraq of jamming devices and all types of electronic interference, but

122

equally on the Iraqi side, Saddam Hussein having himself developed, as early as August 1990, a communication strategy that would finally confuse both the governments of the coalition forces and their military leaders on the ground.

We recall, for example, the analytical and interpretative errors surrounding the damages caused by the first wave of bombers operating in the desert against the renowned Iraqi bunkers, as well as the escape of a large part of Saddam Hussein's air force to the Iranian airports, not to mention the launching sites of the Scud missiles allegedly destroyed at the beginning of the conflict . . .

If there is really a 'victory of Saddam Hussein', it resides above all in the inability of the allies to verify concretely the results of a destructive action of excessive means. As we have seen, a whole panoply of air and space reconnaissance was used, from the AWACS, the JSTAR (Boeing planes equipped with imagery of the terrain for pinpointing the fixed or mobile targets), the Black Hawk helicopters, the whole gamut of drones and other RPVs (Remotely Piloted Vehicles) and, finally, the impressive network of satellites already mentioned.

Despite the networking and thus the possibilities for cross-checking all sources of information at the heart of the installations in the C^3I centres, the electronic command posts where the data was analysed in near-real time in order of priority, then to be implemented by a unique command charged with the whole of air operations (with objectives assigned to aircraft of different forces of the coalition under an integrated military command), the allies could not achieve an exact evaluation of military actions. The uncertainty over their practical results remained total, or nearly so, with the exception of the destruction or neutralization of the adversary's surveillance and guidance radar during the first hours, constituting one of the essential factors of victory.

Another element played equally to the disadvantage of the coalition forces: namely, the extreme difficulty of coordinating the land and air operations on a grand scale; in particular, the conditions of the massive deployment of attack helicopters, where certain analysts raised questions about the training methods of the pilots in the wake of friendly-fire incidents among the allies: 'Might not the excessive number of hours in the simulator contribute to a distorted perception of operational realities?'[7]

Be that as it may, disinformation, active or passive, will have played a decisive role in this experimental war, and the air and space superiority of the allies could not overcome the nebulous uncertainty of the results of combat missions. Among the great powers this would have further repercussions for the means of information destined for civilians, and thus for public opinion.

Therefore, the first of the *ruses de guerre* is no longer a more or less ingenious stratagem, but *an abolition of the appearance of facts*. From now on the defeat of facts [*la défaite des faits*] precedes that of arms: it is less important today to come up with a brilliant manoeuvre, an intelligent tactic, than strategically to cover up information, genuine knowledge, by a process of dissimulation or of disinformation that is less special effect, a known [*avéré*] lie, than *the very abolition of the principle of truth* [*vérité*].

Faced with the erosion of territorial space brought about by the conquest of orbital space, geostrategy and geopolitics will in tandem enter into the artifice of a regime of false temporality, where the TRUE and the FALSE will soon become obsolete, the ACTUAL and the VIRTUAL progressively taking their place, to the great detriment of public credulity . . .

Dissimulating the future in the ultra-short duration of live television, intensive time thus replaces in importance that extensive time where the future was still laid out in the long duration of weeks and months to come. The duel of the offensive and the defensive thus loses its actuality, the attack and the riposte tend to be confused in a *techno-logistical* mix where decoys and countermeasures never cease to proliferate, soon becoming autonomous, while the image itself becomes a high-performance weapon more effective than that which it was supposed to represent.

In the face of *this fusion of the object and its image equivalent*,[8] this confusion of presentation and representation (optical, radar, thermal or acoustic), the procedures of deception in real time prevail over the land, sea and air weapons systems.

The *conflict of interpretation* of the very reality of combat thus changes in nature. The diverse processes of control and interdiction of the battlefield rest less on the state of the opposing forces on the ground than on the state of information and of the instantaneous communication of data. Thus, the importance of the rapid discrimination of targets is really no longer a matter of distinguishing between 'true' [*vrai*] and 'false' carriers of arms (terrestrial or aerial), but between a genuine and false radar signature, a plausible

125

[*vraisemblable*] or implausible acoustic, thermal or electro-optical 'image'.

Thus, in the era of simulated training of military missions, we enter the age of a generalized dissimulation, including the concealment of forces under the terrestrial or marine surfaces (consider, in this regard, the deterrent capacity of nuclear submarines). The war of images and sounds tends to supplement the war of projectiles of the military arsenal. If the Latin root of the word *secret* signifies 'to separate', to separate from understanding, at present this 'separation' is less that of the classic 'distance of space' than that of 'distances of time'. Fooling the adversary about the *durée*, making secret the image of the arms' trajectory, is now more useful than the destructive capacities of the weaponry. Fooling the enemy about the virtuality of the projectile's flight, about the very credibility of its presence here or there, becomes more critical than deceiving the enemy about the reality of its existence. From this comes this generation of stealth weaponry, of undetectable, or nearly undetectable, discrete vehicles, whose employment in the Gulf War will have been a deciding factor.

Two years prior to this conflict, Henri Martre, the head of Aérospatiale, made a prediction: 'The evolution of components and of miniaturization is going to determine the material of tomorrow. *It's the electronics that risk destroying the reliability of a weapon.*'

In effect, if the victor of this last war was indeed the one who knew best how to exploit the electromagnetic spectrum, it is essential that from now on we should consider that the real environment of all important military action is no longer so much the geographic environment, be it desert or other terrain, but rather that of the electromagnetic domain, this dromosphere of waves that are propagated at the speed of elementary particles and permit an instant perception beyond the visible domain, thanks to the different systems of 'trans-horizon' weapons.

_____

Remember, the Royal Observer Corps was originally a civil corps, and did not become part of the British Army, by royal decision, until 1941. Late to be recognized as the principal function of the anti-aircraft force, the function of detection by eye had thus to wait for the beginnings of the Blitz to enter officially the history of the army; while the invention of the first radar during the same epoch highlighted the decisive strategic importance of detection, and thus of early warning, for an island subject to incessant bombings.

Today, where *'All is governed by lightning'* (Heraclitus), the surprising power of instant illumination comes to supplement the observer's capacities of discernment and, as the video photographer Gary Hill declares, *'vision is no longer the possibility of seeing, but the impossibility of not seeing'*.

Totally overexposed to the different sources of intelligence, the electronic battlefield therefore finds that the traditional ballistic procedures of its various projectiles is coupled with an immaterial electromagnetic ballistics of all kinds of data and information circulating without delay in the ether; the precision of the guidance of the weapons'

127

trajectory becomes more important than the explosive charge of the object, intelligent munitions, tele-guided bomb or missiles.

The fateful geographic confusion of the local and the global tends towards the requirement of a sort of generalized feedback of engaged military action; the Global Feedback that the American system implemented to position precisely the vectors of the coalition's air and land weaponry during the Gulf War will prove to have been a prophetic model.

The Global Positioning System, as it is named, enables a rigorous orchestration of operations through the American satellite network. But above all it provides a perfectly automatic equivalence of positioning and tracking of weapons and *matériel* engaged in any air–land conflict whose global scope requires a guidance system, a reliable inertial navigation, to avoid provoking a veritable catalogue of disasters whose impact on public opinion would have been politically unacceptable. As it happens, we remember the tragic error of the bunker in Baghdad occupied by civilians, as well as the Khafji 'friendly fire' scandal that discredited the pilots of the Apache helicopters responsible for this error.

We also observe troubling analogies between the methods of marketing, the organization of industrial and commercial production, and those of the centralized management of the electronic battlefield. First golden rule: *the continuous monitoring of the market*, this obsessive attention that is concerned with the subjective perception of the consumer, that demands, in the military domain this time, a system of advance alert whose installation, during the first months of the Iraqi–Kuwaiti 'business' [*affaire*], allowed for the results with which we are familiar — *the Gulf Crisis could lead only to the victory of Desert Storm.*

Second rule: the organization of just-in-time and zero-stock production: that is to say, the very immediacy of the control and distribution of products — a perfect example of which is the Japanese automobile market — shows up again in the absolute 'geostrategic' control of the Near East battlefield, where flux and just-in-time shooting are confounded thanks to Global Feedback, as we have just seen. Henceforth, *situational reconnaissance* prevails in the industrial and military domains over that of any particular question, the immediacy of telecommunication favouring the globalization of all economic and political action.

Hence this *sudden militarization of mass information* of which we were, for six months, the unconscious victims. This, as well as the attention, also obsessive, that the leaders of the Pentagon focused, via CNN, on the *subjective perception* of the passive consumers of images we had become with this 'live war', where the usual treatment of facts [*faits*] by the press was giving way to the maltreatment [*méfaits*] of the press by a draconian control of news from the front.

But to better understand the promotional innovation of this Gulf Conflict, we must return to a neglected law: that the line of least resistance, or perhaps of least action, governs all technical or scientific innovation. In fact, at the same moment that the *law of mechanical proximity* that had served to manage territories (the environment exogenous to the human species) gives way to a *law of electromagnetic proximity* (become dominant by virtue of its very speed), it is imperative to reconsider the nature of the new 'proximity', this definitive loss of any interval of time and space to the advantage of the interval of absolute speed.

As the revolution of *transports* is coupled with that of *transmissions*, we are already witness to the conditions of the third revolution, that of *transplantations*, thanks to the implantation of interactive components, not only in programmed robots but also in human bodies equipped to control their endogenous environment with the aid of bio-technologies, those stimulators predicted by the cardiac pacemaker.

Not content to reduce to nothing the interval of space and time of all action with telecommunications in real time, the introduction, the transplantation of the weaponry of means of perception and communication to the very interior (following the example of cruise missiles), does away with the usual distinction between *inside* and *outside*, bringing about a discrete fusion between the *exterior space*, where the conflict unfolds, and the *interior space* of the machine; war no longer unfolds only in the external and geographic field of action but, first of all, in the absence of a field, in the guts of the engine of destruction, the *real space* of the arm's technical configuration ceding supremacy to the *real time* of so-called interactive measures. And from this arise the so-called *countermeasures* that attack, if you will, the integrated electronic circuits of the opposing weaponry, and to which the notions of *offensive* and *defensive* no longer apply: the very instantaneity of the interaction of the beams of electro-magnetic radiation no longer pertaining to the strategic measures or usual tactics of action and reaction.

After this, the *law of least action* becomes itself insufficient,

130

since it is henceforth the paradoxical absence of all percepti-
ble action that prevails over the customary activity of attack
or defence; the 'input' and 'output' of data consequently
succeed the classical terms of 'retreat' and 'attack' . . .

Whence a third golden rule common to both war and
'post-industrial' commerce: *one must innovate to conquer.*
Technological innovation thus becomes the principal weapon
of competitions that are as much strategic as economic. The
Gulf War thus amounted to a trade fair of new material, a
'shadow market' for an arms race, where the conquest of
the market is henceforth confused with that of a military
supremacy, where the strategic territories and bases
formerly so coveted are no longer of any interest except as
training grounds, the parade grounds for the laboratories of
the arsenals of post-deterrence East–West. Henceforth
binary deterrence is replaced by the catastrophic conditions of
a *multipolar deterrence*: as the threat of atomic weapons
decreases and the proliferation of non-conventional armaments increases, the field is left open to the primacy of a
third and last system of weaponry no longer *radioactive* but
interactive and every bit as formidable.

Let us indicate here that we should not confuse, as do
certain analysts of military issues, a strategy with an unfinished symphony. The very unfinished character of the 'ex-
centric' Gulf Conflict signals the advent in history of the
supremacy of weapons of communication over weapons of
mass destruction; the hazardous beginnings of a new type of
political deterrence, where the means of mass communication will have an essential role to play in the life of nations
dominated by 'extraterrestrial' technologies, where the

régime of temporality specific to communication devices will *enslave*[9] populations that have become supernumerary. Even if this latest stage of enslavement of man to machine no longer exactly recapitulates that of the earlier voluntary servitude, the loss of the immediate contact induced by tele-technologies will lead to a similar social frustration.

Meanwhile, the series of exoduses to which we are today powerless witnesses signals this sudden transformation of a domestic enslavement of which we, even in Europe, will probably soon be consenting victims.

Concerning the recent migration of the Kurd populations, Danielle Mitterrand stated on 4 April 1991 that 'To displace several million people in order to put them in camps, without employment or liberty, is intolerable; it is like playing the game of Saddam Hussein who declared nearly all of the opposition in his country out of bounds.' One could say the same of those Vietnamese or Cambodians, long forgotten in their camps and their distress, while tomorrow or the day after it could be the Russians or Yugoslavians.

Behind these media-staged strategic events [*stratégico-médiatique*], we observe another form of panic induced by the very spectacle of the false proximity of *live* news. I want to speak about this little-analysed phenomenon of those 'tourists of desolation' who suddenly leave the fine arable lands of European regions of temperate climate – unlike the escapees of the Sahel and of Africa now turned into desert – to fly like moths towards the television glow of a consumer society that inevitably fails to meet their expectations, as with those Albanians embarking for the south of Italy, where there is rampant unemployment in the order of 60 per cent of the population of Apulia.

Yesterday, *tourists on a pleasure trip*, with the rise of the transportation revolution and the popularization of the automobile. Today, *tourists on a 'trip'* [*déplacement*] *without hope of return*, with the development of the revolution of broadcasting and those audiovisual vehicles that give something – it matters not what – to see and hear, and thus induce the mass exodus of people tricked by the illusion of an electromagnetic mirage.

While waiting for this third revolution, that of every kind of stimulator transplantation, where each will be able to 'shoot up' here and now, without having to move physically, thanks to the pernicious effects of the virtual space of an electronic drug that will extend the effects of chemical drugs, and thus favour all 'separatisms', since, according to Heraclitus, 'those who sleep are in separate worlds, while those awake are in the same world'.

Let us return now, by way of conclusion, to this threat to democracy that is constituted in the tyranny of *real time: how to share power when the time in which it manifests itself escapes us?*

How can we hope to control decisions that escape not only us by virtue of their speed but also escape their 'authors' by the very automatism of the material that makes these decisions for them?

Already, the 'fourth power' dissolves in the procedures of instantaneous information for which nobody is truly responsible, the notions of MEDIA and MEDIATION tend themselves to disappear in a short circuit, a feedback that definitively nullifies the necessary independence of the news, especially its rational interpretation.

133

And so the formidable spectre of a 'fourth front' looms up on the horizon, where weapons of communication would no longer have anything in common with our current means of information and whose purely technical imperialism will come with a return of a feudalism where the old dungeon of the lords of the land would be advantageously replaced by the satellite, master of both the space and time of societies enslaved to their customary control, meteorology having been but a foreshadowing of the planetary regulation of humanity . . .

Since these new 'weapons of communications' have the privilege to serve − in all impunity − just as much in times of peace as in times of declared war, we can easily imagine the risks of such an orbital deployment of power to democratic control. A crucial question arises at this precise instant in history: *can one democratize ubiquity, instantaneity, omniscience and omnipresence*, which are precisely the privileges of the divine, or in other words, of autocracy?

Such is indeed the question that presents itself, from the present day forward, to those who would construct 'the global village', this tele-topic meta-city whose appearance none can yet guess, nor whose destiny glimpse.

The unique merit of the Persian Gulf War will therefore have been that of summoning us to respond politically to the challenge of real time, whose fault we will soon see arise in comparison with mystical fundamentalism, a delirious technical fundamentalism, a new illuminism whose ravages will soon be upon us.

1 June 1991

V

Virilio Looks Back and Sees the Future: Interview by James Der Derian (2000)

JD: Why the title, *Desert Screen*?

PV: The screen is the site of *projection of the light of images* — MIRAGES of the geographic desert like those of the CINEMA. It is also the site of *projections of the force of energy* — beginning with the desert in New Mexico, the first atomic explosion at the Trinity site, and leading up to the Persian Gulf War when *the screens of the Kuwaiti and Iraqi deserts* were to be linked with the *television screens* of the entire world, thanks to CNN. As for the poliorcetic, the fortifications, let us not forget the idea of the GLACIS, the clearing of the depth of the *field of vision* beyond the ramparts, that for the defenders provided an advantage over their attackers — this NO-MAN'S LAND that is finally the other meaning of the desert: 'The greatest glory of a state being, according to the Romans, to make its frontiers a vast desert.'

JD: Seven years before the Gulf War, you wrote *War and Cinema*. I must now ask: does war imitate art?

PV: War is in every way an art, a *theatre of operation* where stratagems are essential to deceive the enemy (and the allies) with respect to the action taking place — and from this come the terms for the dissimulating tactics of war [*ruse de guerre*]: camouflage, disinformation . . . But above all, the *field of battle* is a *field of perception* which must be organized in such a way as to control the movements of the adversary and cause them to follow a false lead, to demoralize them and exterminate them. From this arises the strategic role for the dominant position: the hill or the lookout tower and later of the *telescope*, anticipating aerial reconnaissance, radar, spy satellites and today drones.

Thanks to the animated image, to talking pictures and above all to generalized tele-surveillance, war has moved from the geographic *field of battle* to the multimedia *field of vision*. A perfect example is that of the spectacular terrorism of the Palestinians by which they first captured the *television screens* of the whole world — specifically, the dramas of 'black September' in Jordan, and the symbolic attack on the Olympic Games in Munich — before regaining *territories* . . . without speaking of the more recent role of the *intifada* at the moment of the opening of the Camp David negotiations.

JD: You write in *Desert Screen* of the first total electronic war, of the matter of the body disappearing in the process. Are there ethical implications?

PV: Previously, wars were MATTER WARS, wars of *matériel*. Troops of legions, of divisions, of tanks and various armadas dominated battle, and this from antiquity right up to the great modern wars. Since the era of nuclear deterrence, however, international war has become a LIGHT WAR that illustrates Heraclitus' words whereby 'everything obeys lightning', that is, obeys the real time of an instantaneous interactivity that no longer allows for a distinction, as once was the case, between offence and defence, but also, between the *inside* and *outside* of the real space of confrontations. After having been *local* and then *total*, war tends henceforth to become not only *global* but above all GLO-CAL and delocalized, like post-industrial businesses from the era of the global economy. But if people lose much of their demographic importance in international conflicts, they nonetheless retain this advantage in ever multiplying civil wars. Finally, we can even speak in the literal sense, that a *war of zero casualties* is an inhuman war, or transhuman war, and that *immaterial war*, pure war, is only ever an 'ecological accident', the fruit of the extreme development of our techno-sciences.

JD: Who won the Gulf War? Who lost?

PV: Here we are faced with a transpolitical paradox: he who was defeated (Saddam Hussein) did not lose the war, since he remains in power and retains his potential for harm. The *war of zero casualties* (or nearly, on the side of the allies) was therefore also a *war of zero political victory* ... After the *cold* war between the East and West, *hot* war no longer results in the elimination of the enemy's power. We have just verified this once more, ten years later, in the Balkans.

JD: What then is the future of war? Something like the Gulf and Kosovo? Or more like Mogadishu and Rwanda? Hand to hand? Or machine against machine?

PV: According to Clausewitz, 'War is the pursuit of politics by other means.' Henceforth, 'The (full-scale) accident is the prolongation of (total) war by other means.'

In effect, if yesterday, in *material wars*, SUBSTANCE was absolutely necessary and the ACCIDENT relative and contingent, in the *immaterial wars* of tomorrow we will witness a strategic reversal, since the *accident* will become ABSOLUTE (ecologically) and SUBSTANCE (all substances) RELATIVE and

CONTINGENT. From these circumstances we are likely to witness the surpassing of *military* war by a catastrophic endemic of a *civil* war approaching global scale, as was previously the case in the twentieth century with *military* war between the great nations. Consider, by way of confirmation, the following point made by the supreme commander of NATO, General William Kernan, in August 2000: 'Henceforth NATO will fight illegal immigration, ethnic violence and international crime.'

JD: Is human intervention possible? Preferable?

PV: In fact, man is no longer the *centre of the world* of anthropocentrism or geocentrism; he has become, in the course of the twentieth century, the *end of the world* of a technoscientific nihilism. 'The man of war' is no longer a soldier but rather a thinker, he who invents and programs weapons of destruction. A phrase illustrates this point: 'We generally believe that AUTOMATION does away with the possibility of human error. In fact, it transfers this possibility from the level of action to the level of conception and development.'[1] Finally, Reagan's 'Star Wars' or the 'National Missile Defense' of Clinton and Bush are just the same: the catastrophic development of a *conceptual accident*! In the course of the last century, *this merciless century* as Camus called it, we expected *war* or *revolution*. During the coming century, we must expect the *accident*! A 'full-scale accident' [*accident intégral*] that will be for the TRANSPOLITICAL politics of liberalism what the 'great night' was yesterday for the TRANSHISTORICAL politics of communism.

JD: Today, military schools are studying Virilio's works. Is this of consequence?

PV: Military professors really ought to study the Bible, the Old Testament, where Joshua stopped the sun . . . or even the New Testament, the Apocalypse of John.

Notes

I FOREWORD

1. 'The Influence of Weaponry on History'. Published in Paris by Payot. [Tr.]
2. Force of rapid action. [Tr.]
3. J. F. C. Fuller, *La Guerre mécanique et ses applications*. Paris: Éditions Berger-Levrault, 1948, p. 30.
4. Virilio's neologism *satellitaire* is less awkward than its English equivalent. [Tr.]
5. Virilio's use of the word is alluding to the Greek term for military leader, *strategos*. [Tr.]
6. This refers to the deterrence doctrine that targeted populations as opposed to military targets (counter-force strategies). [Tr.]
7. See Nicole Loraux, 'L'autochtonie, une topique athénienne', *Les Annales*, January–February, 1979.
8. The word *stasis* in Greek refers to taking a defiant *stand* in a civil uprising. [Tr.]
9. The French phrase *droit de cité* preserves more closely the definitional role of the *polis* in determining citizens' rights. [Tr.]
10. *Nomos* is Greek for 'law' or 'custom'. Virilio is developing here the derivation of the word *nomos* from its root *nemo* [νέμω], which entails notions of habitation and the delimitation of territory. [Tr.]
11. The Roman foot soldier. [Tr.]
12. Deriving originally from the Greek word *pneuma*, 'wind' or 'spirit', this term's primary meaning in French is 'spiritual'. [Tr.]
13. In the autumn of 1990, a computer was installed in the Pentagon

in Washington in order to manage the Gulf Crisis. The name of this *deus ex machina*: the 'inertial center'.

14. The reference is to the second year of the French Revolutionary calendar, which was the official calendar of France between 24 November 1793 and 31 December 1805. [Tr.]

15. An allusion to the blue helmets worn by UN peacekeepers. [Tr.]

16. This text of pseudo-Xenophon can be found in L. Canfora's book, *La démocratie comme violence*, Desjonquères, 1989.

17. Roman cavalry. [Tr.]

18. The trireme was an ancient Greek vessel with three rows of oars. [Tr.]

II AUGUST 1990: DESERT SHIELD

1. We shall retain the French here (*durée*), as there is no satisfactory way of rendering the term in English that consistently retains the field of associations so important to Virilio's arguments. While the term means essentially a span or lapse of time, an 'extent' of time, it has a more formal, abstract force in the French that Virilio is employing in particularly important theoretical ways throughout the book. As such, it is often paired with *l'étendue*, or 'extension', as the abstract formal term for the measure of the extent or expanse of space. [Tr.]

2. Here we see the quintessential pairing of the abstract terms denoting time and space, *la durée* and *l'étendue*, which lies at the theoretical basis of the various instances of *durée* that have been preserved throughout the book. [Tr.]

3. Farewell address of President Carter to the American nation, which Virilio has paraphrased. The actual text of the passage is as follows: 'In an all-out nuclear war, more destructive power than in all of World War II would be unleashed every second during the long afternoon it would take for all the missiles and bombs to fall.

A World War II every second – more people killed in the first few
hours than all the wars of history put together.' [Tr.]

4. Conférence sur la sécurité et la coopération en Europe. [Tr.]
5. 'A Woman on the Moon'. [Tr.]
6. Virilio is playing on two senses of the word *remonter*, 'to go
   back', as in a time-machine trip back in time, and 'to edit' in
   cinematography (seen just above). [Tr.]
7. 'Aesop stays here and rests.' [Tr.]

III JANUARY 1991: DESERT STORM

1. The Greek is *hubris* (Heraclitus, fr. 43). [Tr.]
2. The French term is a literal translation of *Blitzkrieg*, 'lightning
   war'. [Tr.]
3. *Le Nouvel Observateur*, 13–14 January 1991.
4. The original phrase *trouble de la perception* is used to name the
   visual disorders of both colour blindness and synaesthesia. [Tr.]
5. A lustrum is a period of five years. [Tr.]
6. The Belinograph was a portable facsimile machine capable of
   using ordinary telephone lines that was invented by Edouard
   Belin in 1913. [Tr.]
7. A system of simultaneous communication of two or more
   messages on the same wire or radio channel. [Tr.]
8. The full slogan, as recorded in Parisian graffiti of 1968, *Il est
   interdit d'interdire*, literally 'It is prohibited to prohibit!', is
   comparable to the English counter-culture slogan 'Down with
   authority'. [Tr.]
9. The term employed here, *dissuasive*, as in *dissuasion*, 'deterrence', could thus also be translated as 'deterrent'. [Tr.]
10. The Paris air show held in Bourget. [Tr.]
11. Virilio is playing on a sense of the original Latin (*parare*) that is
    retained in the French but only barely in the English 'parry'.

The *Oxford English Dictionary*'s second entry for the etymology of the word is: 'to prepare to receive (a blow), to ward off, defend, cover, shield'. Virilio is thus referring at once to the muster of garb and guard. [Tr.]

12. A. J. Toynbee, *Guerre et civilisation*, Paris: Gallimard, 1953.

13. *La guerre des machines à la guerre des poitrines*. [Tr.]

14. Toynbee, *Guerre et civilisation*.

15. More or less continuous zones of boundary fortifications constructed during the Roman empire. [Tr.]

16. Service d'information et de relations publiques des armées, the French army public information service. [Tr.]

17. 'A Parallel History'. A documentary series on Arte that showed propaganda and newsreel footage from the Second World War, grouped by event or battle or date, from every side – German, English, French, American, Russian – hence, in 'parallel'. [Tr.]

18. The reference is to the *agitki* newsreels created for the purpose of agitation and propaganda during the Bolshevik revolution that were distributed throughout Russia on specially equipped trains, called agit-trains. [Tr.]

19. The phrase refers to the day, 10 November 1630, that Louis XIII renewed his confidence in Richelieu to the surprise of all, and that by extension signifies a circumstance in which events turn in an unanticipated direction. [Tr.]

20. The AFP trial/Pentagon. AFP refers to the Agence France-Presse. [Tr.]

21. Virilio is playing here on the phrase designating the 'standing army' by exploiting its literal meaning, the 'great mute'. [Tr.]

22. The word *allô* with which the French answer the phone differs from the more casual English greeting 'hello', as it is used solely in responding to the call, as Virilio notes, of the *appareil*, the 'instrument'. [Tr.]

23. The acronym adopted by Community Antenna Television, the first US home cable utility.

IV JUNE 1991: DESERT SCREEN

1. A perfect example of this tele-action which completes television.
2. The neologism is derived from the Greek terms *eikon*, 'semblance', 'likeness', and *dynamis*, 'power'. [Tr.]
3. The avionics of a plane represent its entire electronic equipment.
4. During the Gulf Conflict, the Agence France-Presse brought a legal suit against the Pentagon, which had refused to include them in the media pool.
5. Pierre Kohler, 'L'Électronique dans la guerre', *Science et avenir*, March 1991.
6. One remembers the problems with the Hubble telescope: it was 'myopic' because certain American technologies of the utilization of the famous mirrors had been classified top secret.
7. Bernard Bombeau, 'Spécial Golfe', *Aviation Magazine*, March 1991.
8. Research into the smallest 'radar signature' is at the base of so-called 'stealth' technology.
9. Virilio's use of the term *asservir*, which means not only to 'enslave' but also to operate a machine by remote control, persists in the subsequent references to enslavement. [Tr.]

V VIRILIO LOOKS BACK AND SEES THE FUTURE: INTERVIEW BY JAMES DER DERIAN (2000)

1. Citation from Nigel Calder, ed., *Unless Peace Comes*. London: Allen Lane/Penguin Press, 1968.

Index